More of
Life and Love

Msgr. Jim Lisante

Resurrection Press
An Imprint of
CATHOLIC BOOK PUBLISHING CORP.
Totowa • New Jersey

Grateful acknowledgment is made to *The Long Island Catholic* to reproduce essays contained in these pages.

First published in August 2010 by
Catholic Book Publishing/Resurrection Press
77 West End Road
Totowa, NJ 07512

ISBN 978-1-933066-14-1
Library of Congress Catalog Card Number: 2010928256

Cover design by Beth DeNapoli
Cover photo and photo on p. 8 by Lisa Jandovitz

Printed in the United States of America

Contents

Dedication

As this book is published, we happily approach the 90th birthday of my beloved Mom, Cecelia.

So let me dedicate this book to her. A woman of faith, boundless love, uplifting humor, a seemingly unlimited kindness and the best Mom any children could have.

At night, shortly after getting her to bed, one of my favorite sights is finding her busily in prayerful conversation with her God. I'm so glad they're such close friends! And eternally grateful to her and my Dad Nicholas for planting the life-giving grace of an active and lived faith.

I love you, Mom. Now and always.

Msgr. Jim Lisante and Jonathan Jackson

Foreword

I FIRST met Msgr. Jim Lisante in New York in the summer of 2000. I was scheduled, along with my brother, to be interviewed by him. I have to confess, he was the first priest I had ever had a conversation with—and I was eighteen years old at the time. Not knowing what to expect, I was subconsciously contending with a series of unknown and undesired prejudices: *Is this guy going to act like a human, or some kind of religious zombie? Does he really know the love of God, or is he simply devoted to a system? Is he going to ask my opinion on some obscure, controversial doctrine?*

Well, in about one minute's time, all of those fears were dispelled and I was having an amazing conversation with one of the most sincere Christians I had ever met. If every priest was like Jim Lisante, the whole world might be Catholic! That one interview has extended into a genuine friendship—one of which I am extremely thankful for.

I have had the privilege of knowing Jim Lisante for over ten years now, and I can speak from personal experience that he is a man who walks in profound love and wisdom—a man of deep faith, immense joy, and tremendous humor.

More of Life and Love is inundated with spiritual insights and personal stories from a man who lives the Gospel day in and day out. One of Jim Lisante's secrets, I believe, is that he truly understands relationships and how to connect with the heart. He masterfully places the *ideas* of truth in the context of personal experiences, and by doing so, transforms mere concepts into relational realities that draw the reader closer to the heart and purpose of God. Another secret, is that he actually loves people; he doesn't just talk about it—and this genuine desire for the ultimate good of the other person, naturally illuminates the pages of this book. He also walks the often difficult but sacred balance of Grace and Truth with astonishing precision and care. He is unafraid to speak the truth; but always does so with mercy and grace at the forefront of his vision.

Jim Lisante creatively draws on the brilliance of Jesus by means of pictures, stories, and parables to communicate the complexity of God's nature. He uses humorous stories as well as tragic ones, to open up our hearts to the wondrous gift that *life* and *love* really are.

What you have in your hands is a treasure chest of divine wisdom and experiences from a soul who lives and breathes the mysterious love of God. I am honored and blessed to recommend this book to anyone who is searching the heart of God on important matters of faith. I am confident that your spirit will be inspired, challenged, and uplifted by the radiant expressions of God's goodness, working in and through this incredible servant of Christ.

Msgr. Lisante is a true Father—but he gains his strength from allowing himself to rest in the beautiful intimacy of a much-loved child! Here is a man who knows a thing or two about *life* and *love*!

Listen closely and rejoice!

Jonathan Jackson

Actor, Musician, Filmmaker, and Author

April 25, 2010

Part I

More of
Life

The Pro-Life Vision of Frank Capra

Each year at Christmas our televisions seem packed with specials to celebrate the season. Beyond doubt, the most popular film during this holiday is a 1946 classic called *It's a Wonderful Life*. Directed by filmmaker Frank Capra (who died in 1991), it stars Jimmy Stewart, Donna Reed and Lionel Barrymore.

The movie tells the story of a man named George Bailey. He is filled with dreams and hopes and possibilities in his youth. He wants to travel, to experience life fully, to be a success, to collect many possessions, to have a good time.

But throughout his life he has to make choices between what's selfish and what's selfless. And these choices mean that his dreams often evaporate. Because when you choose to walk through the door of goodness and giving, you also close other doors that might lead to personal pleasure. George chooses to live for others and sometimes the giving causes him to "burn out."

One night, on Christmas Eve, his spirits are particularly low. He contemplates suicide. He believes that death would be preferable to living for others. Enter Clarence, George's guardian angel. Clarence helps George to see the richness in living for others. He shows George what life (for others) would have been like, had he never been born. And through this experience George comes to see that a life lived with generosity, with compassion, and with selflessness, is not only a wonderful life, but the only life worth living.

When we watch this delightful film, it's easy to get into feeling good, feeling sentimental and missing the great power this movie has to challenge us. Pope John Paul II said that we are on this planet to be "signs of contradiction" to a world which rejects the values of Jesus.

George Bailey is that contradiction. He's a person who celebrates a family life. He's faithful to his wife. And she's clearly

10

a partner who is his best friend. They see children as a blessing, not a burden. As a family, their feelings are expressed openly and honestly, even the disagreements. The Baileys also pray; they're not afraid to openly express their reliance on God.

Not all the Baileys are perfect. Like every family, they have problems, but the problematic member is loved, not denied. Uncle Billy, for example, is clearly an eccentric, a kind but befuddled man. The Baileys never mistreat this confused relation. They attempt, through patience and love, to fill in where Uncle Billy is lacking. In all that the Baileys do they reflect a belief in the sacredness of human life. In many ways, this forties film is prophetic. It celebrates the life forces presently under siege. It affirms family, children, the poor, the elderly, the infirm and the outcasts of society.

Capra, as he aged, recognized that his favorite film stood in direct opposition to the values of our culture. And in explaining the vision of *It's a Wonderful Life*, he said:

"It was my kind of film for my kind of people. A film to tell the weary, the disheartened, and the disillusioned, the wino, the junkie, the prostitute, those behind prison walls and those behind iron curtains, that no man is a failure!

"To show those born slow of foot or slow of mind, those oldest sisters condemned to spinsterhood, and those oldest sons condemned to unschooled toil, that each man's life touches so many other lives. And that if he isn't around it would leave an awful hole.

"A film that said to the downtrodden, the pauper, 'Heads up, fella. No man is poor who has one friend. Three friends and you're filthy rich.'

"A film that expressed its love for the homeless and the loveless; for those whose cross is heavy and him whose touch is ashes; for the Magdalenes stoned by hypocrites and the afflicted Lazaruses with only dogs to lick their sores.

"I wanted to shout to the abandoned grandfathers staring vacantly in nursing homes, to the always-interviewed but seldom-adopted halfbreed orphans, to the paupers who refuse to die while medical vultures wait to snatch their hearts and livers, and to those who take cobalt treatments and whistle—I wanted to shout, 'You are the salt of the earth, and *It's a Wonderful Life* is my memorial to you!' "

Even after several serious strokes, weak as he sometimes was, his love of life, his concern for the unborn and the born never ebbed. He delighted in the knowledge that, long after he had gone home to God, his film would continue to proclaim, with incredible clarity, that every single life is a limitless gift from God, and that ours is a wonderful life!

Question for Reflection

- How has a recent movie reinforced the lessons that George Baily learned in *It's a Wonderful Life*?

January 22nd

Tommy called at around 5 p.m. "Hey, Father Jim, what are you doing tonight, want to hang out?" "Can't tonight," I responded. "I have to head East to give a pro-life talk. Do you want to come?" "Sure, beats staying home." And so off we went, stopping for a quick burger on the way. Tommy is 16. He is a non-stop talker, an attractive kid in personality and looks. A "success" with the opposite sex, he (like many teenagers) talks about "hitting on" girls a lot of the time. He is charming and somewhat irresponsible, and, like many of his peers, not very much in touch with the consequences of his actions.

I spoke that night to a group of young adults and their parents. Then they watched the powerful film produced by Dr. Bernard N. Nathanson called *The Silent Scream*. The movie, put together by a man who used to do abortions, simply shows what an abortion looks like. People complain that the film is hard to take. So is abortion.

When the lights in the auditorium came back on there was a stillness you could cut with a knife. The only sound heard was some sniffles. A dialogue then began. One teacher was obviously angry. She thought the film too emotional, too graphic. She was countered by a 17-year-old girl who stood to say, "Maybe we need real life pictures," and then she went on to say what truly matters; "I never really thought about what I would do if I became pregnant, but after seeing this movie I know that abortion could never be one of my choices."

During the ride home my talkative friend Tommy was uncharacteristically silent. Finally, several miles into our journey, he spoke. "Father Jim, you know I had sex a few times and I never really worried about it. I mean, I always figured that if anything happened I could always, you know, have it taken care of . . . but that movie wiped me out. I never thought of it as a real kid before. How can people do that?"

They do it, Tommy, because they too have been conned into forgetting that beyond talk of "a woman's body," or "personal choice," or "reproductive freedom," the life destroyed is a human person of infinite value and potential. Most people are not evil; they are ignorant. Abortion has become a word without meaning. Tommy is like most people I meet. They have anesthetized themselves to a very uncomfortable reality. They have allowed abortion to become just another word for problem-solver.

Each January 22nd many of us gather in Washington, D.C., to walk for life. We are there as a way to say to a nation of Tommys: Please realize what is happening in America. Please know that we are destroying our own future. We are there to commemorate that day in 1973, when the Supreme Court, in a wildly flawed decision, said that a baby in utero has no right to life. In marching we hope to effect a change in the law, but for the immediate moment our hope is much simpler: to remind Americans today considering abortion that the choice for life is theirs.

Remember several years ago the horror and revulsion we all shared when ABC television's *The Day After* showed us the effects of nuclear war? Well, imagine this comparative tragedy: a terrible force is unleashed. It decimates the populations of Montana, North and South Dakota, Wyoming, Colorado, Kansas, Minnesota, Iowa, Oregon, Idaho and Nebraska. You see, that is how many Americans we have lost through abortion since 1973—lives of infinite value known now only to God.

As we sadly remember and reflect on these years of senseless death, it might be good to consider the words of Dr. Nathanson in the closing moments of his film *The Silent Scream*. This modern St. Paul, who likewise persecuted and destroyed the beloved of our Lord, expressed the rationale for his conversion about unborn life this way: "Since the 1960s we have a science which is known as fetology, which has allowed us to study the human fetus. And all of those studies have concluded without exception that the unborn child is a human being, indistinguishable from any of us and an integral part of our human community.

"Now, the destruction of a living human being is no solution to what is basically a social problem. And I believe a resort to such violence is an admission of scientific, and even worse, ethical impoverishment. Somehow I refuse to believe that Americans, who have put men on the moon, can't devise a better solution than the resort to violence.

"I think we should all here and now devote ourselves to an untiring effort to devise a better solution, a solution compounded equally of love, and compassion, and a decent regard for the overriding priority of human life.

"Let's all, for humanity's sake, here and now, stop the killing!"

Question for Reflection

- How does the comparison of the number of Americans lost through abortion to those lost in nuclear war affect you?

"Don't Worry, Be Happy"

Carter Cooper had it all.

He was young, handsome, rich, well-connected, talented and famous. He was the son of Gloria Vanderbilt. He had what most everyone else wants. He had, as the expression goes, everything to live for.

But in July 1988, after battling months of depression and inconsolable interior pain, Carter checked out. In the presence of his pleading and shocked mom, Carter Cooper jumped off the balcony of their 14th floor apartment, falling to an instant death. His pain was, at last, over.

But for the people who loved him, the question of "Why?" would echo time and again.

In his leap to freedom from the emotional and psychic nightmares which robbed him of peace, Carter Cooper joined some 450,000 teenagers and young adults who attempt suicide each year. Somewhere between five and ten thousand young people "succeed." For every completed suicide there is an average of 8 close survivors who are left behind to pick up the pieces.

The incidence of young persons trying to "off" themselves is growing tremendously. The CDC reports that it is the third leading cause of death or youths ages 15 to 24. And the depression that leads to suicide is an "equal opportunity" visitor. The poor, the rich, the middle class—all share in the downward spiral of despair.

In the early Church there were catalogues of serious sin. Certainly murder and sexual promiscuity were high on the list of moral wrongs. But right up there, at the top, was the sin of despair.

The thinking of the Church elders was that if you really believed that Jesus saved us, then there should be no reason to despair. If you believe in the love of God, only rejoicing makes sense.

The problem is, there are a lot of people in our world who aren't so sure they are loved by God or by others. And even if they know that others love them, they have a really tough time loving themselves or allowing the love of others to really touch them.

The Carter Coopers don't just happen. When a young person attempts suicide there are usually reasons or causes for the desperation.

The most common cause is simply a need to escape. So many homes are torn apart by family crisis. We're living in a time with more divorce, separation, addiction, abuse (physical and emotional) and conflict than ever before. And in the middle of all this chaos and hurt, we've got less time to deal with our problems because of the frantic pace at which we lead our lives.

When a person experiences a need in our culture, there are many temporary means we use to achieve immediate and oftentimes superficial gratification. Drinking and drugging come to mind. Sexual release is another temporary remedy to alienation, loneliness or despair.

But the most alluring end to pain or emptiness is sometimes seen as death. It's a way, some believe, to peace. Finally, they reason, the pain will go away. It seems to be an easier way to cope: the sleep of death rather than the struggle of pain, misunderstanding, loss and loneliness.

Sometimes, too, suicide becomes a way to strike back. When I have anger I can't express or people I can't reach, suicide is a way to communicate my frustration. People will, finally, take notice.

What do we do? Suicide is a dead end, and a senseless one at that. It causes us to lose some of the most sensitive souls around us. We need to be aware, before the death alternative is tried, of the warning signs of despair. (And most young persons do let us know that they're heading down that hopeless path.)

First, if someone says they're thinking about suicide, take them seriously. It's not true that the ones who talk about it never do it. They do.

Second, don't believe that only the wild child is thinking about suicide. Suicide happens among the "perfect" teenagers or young adults as often as it does among the drinkers, the drug-users or the school failures. In fact, heightened expectations about how well a person should succeed can set us up for an even greater fall.

Third, watch out for major personality changes. Zany or irrational behavior can be natural parts of growth and development. But huge movements toward dangerous activities, altered appetites, aggression, moodiness or withdrawal should send up red flags. Serious disturbances at home, at school or with the police shouldn't be ignored.

Take the clues seriously. Don't be afraid to seek professional help. Too many families believe that psychological counseling is only for "crazies." The truth is that sane and intelligent people recognize the need for outside help and get it.

Above all, remain calm and non-judgmental. If a son, a daughter or a friend is really depressed and shares those feelings with you, please don't be the dismissive jerk who says, "Well, we all go through that, you'll get over it." Or, "It's wrong to feel that way." Listen, support, affirm and steer the hurting person to those who can help.

Some people who can assist you at times of crisis are The Samaritans. They operate a worldwide 24-hour hotline to aid people in despair. There are over 700 helplines in the United States alone. Go to www.samaritans.org for current information. They really can help.

The fact that America has made Bobby McFerrin's song *Don't Worry, Be Happy* a classic tells us a lot about ourselves.

We really do want our world to be simple; to be happy; to hurt a lot less.

But sometimes, for all the upbeat songs, the pain is too much. Don't ignore the pain. Face it and get help.

Carter Cooper would have loved the song; he just couldn't live it.

Questions for Reflection

- If you were called upon to help someone who was contemplating suicide, what would you do?
- What would you not do or say?

When It Just Hurts Too Much

The recent spate of teenage suicides has been jarring my memory. I reflect back to my high school years and realize that for me, and for many others, they were years of sometimes painful growth.

They were times of disappointment. They were times of struggle with self-esteem. They were times less filled with real love than infatuation. They were definitely times when every personal crisis took on monumental importance. And even though parents, and older friends, and guidance counselors would say, "Don't worry, you'll look back on these times and wonder what all the fuss was about," it didn't diminish the way I felt.

And that was all right, because our feelings are our feelings. They're not right or wrong, they just are. And we're entitled to them. Having someone tell us that what worries us isn't really important doesn't make it any less intense or real.

Having an adult say that our feelings are "adolescent" or "immature" doesn't make us handle our crisis any quicker or better. No, it's probably best to accept the feelings we have and try to work with and through them.

And where the problems and feelings hurt too much, it's definitely best to share them with people who really care.

I got a call a while back from a girl named Janet. She had just turned sixteen. Janet had botched an attempt at suicide and wanted to talk over the forces that drove her to think about ending her life. After many hours the greatest of her needs surfaced: Janet, like the rest of us, needed very badly to be truly loved as a person instead of a thing.

In the year before her suicide attempt, Janet had been involved in two different relationships. Both led to sex. In both cases Janet admits that she thought that having sex would make the guys love her more. In both cases sex was actually followed by feelings of emptiness and of being used.

Janet said that the calls became less frequent after each sexual encounter. The terms of endearment both guys had used to coax Jan into bed were said less often. The attention they paid her generally was much less intense. And most frightening for Janet was a feeling she developed about herself: she came to believe that her only real value was for sex.

The person she was inside—her feelings, her emotions, her sensitivities, her talents—was reduced or eliminated. Her self-image faded with every experience of sex. She was left, having just shared the deepest part of herself with another human being, feeling alone and empty. She said that she could be lying right next to the boyfriend of the moment and still feel an intense isolation which made her want to throw up.

Janet was hurting badly. And she felt that there were no avenues for communicating what she felt. Feeling poorly about herself led her to presume that anyone she spoke to would dislike her too. She was afraid others would judge her or put her down. And she just couldn't handle that. She was imprisoned by feelings of worthlessness and hurt. The pain was just too much.

One day Janet took pills, a lot of them. They almost killed her. Janet had finally given way to despair.

When Janet awoke at the local community hospital she didn't know how to feel. She was shocked to see her parents. They looked hurt, they looked worried, they looked angry, they looked relieved—all at the same time.

They told her that they were hurt that she hadn't felt free enough to confide her troubles to them. They said they were scared and worried because they almost lost a daughter they may not always like or understand, but whom they love very much.

They were also angry because that's how parents respond when they have no better way to express their pain. And they were hopeful, because they knew that they had a chance to try again.

Janet, her self-image and her family needed help. They now get the help they require. They sometimes find themselves wanting to give up because the experience of family counseling isn't always easy. But they don't. And maybe that's the key to the peace and the gentle smile you see on Janet's face more recently.

She knows that people care. She knows that she's not alone. She doesn't have all the answers, but she's no longer terrified of the journey toward self-discovery.

If you're feeling something like Janet—confused, or hurting, or isolated, or that the pain is just too much—please call for help. For suicide prevention information, personal stories and resources go to www.save.org.

There really are people who care. And looking to death instead of for a lifeline is such a tragic waste.

Let people who've walked out of the same darkness be a source of light and hope for you.

Because you matter too much not to.

Questions for Reflection

- Has counseling ever helped you to get through a time of crisis?
- Have you visited the website www.save.org? Share something from it that you found helpful.

"Papa Don't Preach"

Madonna. I have to admit she hasn't always been a favorite of mine. Something about her sacrilegious uses of the cross have troubled many. And her suggestive sexuality somehow always seems just the other side of good taste.

But lately I've been rethinking her value. Remember the hit song *Papa Don't Preach*? It said some pretty important things. And only a star like Madonna could put the values reflected in this song at the top of the charts.

In the song Madonna ponders the plight of a young adult finding herself pregnant before marriage. She's realistic and knows that having and keeping her baby will be tough. She's heard from all her "friends" that she should get rid of it, that she should "give it up." But she loves the life within her body and proclaims, "I'm keeping my baby!"

Her biggest obstacle is her dad. His love for her has always been built around so many "do's" and "don'ts." And now she's committed the biggest "don't" of them all. She shares her fears of his response. She expects him to be both paternalistic and preachy in putting her down.

In this Madonna reflects a common feeling among young people. They need, even in the midst of horrible and challenging life situations, to be accepted and loved. They need our support and tenderness. They don't need to be lectured to about their errors. They know how they've messed up. They need to hear, no matter what, that we're with them through both the mountaintops and the valleys of life experience.

We can, as parents and teachers, love our young with conditions: "I'll love you if, I'll love you when, I'll love you but . . . ." We're challenged by Christ to love without any conditions. That doesn't mean that we can't call our young people to realize their full potential, but it also means that we're unafraid to articulate our love especially when they fail. We are to love always and forever, no matter what.

The song Madonna sings highlights another great truth we sometimes miss: we can all learn a lot about courage and heroism from both our married and unmarried mothers-to-be.

Every day there are women whose ages range from 14 to 40 standing against the tide of popular opinion. They're pregnant, and they're scared. Their friends have oftentimes written them off. They may not have much money. But they know something profoundly important. They know that there's a life in them. They know that this life is precious and unique. And they resent a fact about contemporary existence: that there is presently no place on our planet as unsafe as the womb. And although they won't find it easy to bear and raise a child, they're going to give their children the chance to be—the chance that everyone deserves.

That choice for life makes all mothers pretty courageous and daring people.

When you see an expectant mother, be daring too. Tell her that you think she's great. Tell her congratulations and thanks. Tell her that.

How great it is to think that a song celebrating the courage to give life was the number-one song in our land and is still known many years later.

There is still hope, America! Thanks, Madonna.

Questions for Reflection

- Have you ever thought of pregnant women as courageous and daring?
- How can you show a pregnant friend or relative that you respect their courage?

Is Pro-Choice Really About Choice?

A seminarian classmate died while we were in college. His name was Al Roberts, and he was an incredibly sensitive and caring man. He had a special place in his heart for the handicapped and disabled.

To commemorate him after his tragic departure at 20 years of age his classmates set up a fund to aid the handicapped children he loved. To raise funds we would hold a benefit each year featuring a visit by someone of note. Wonderful people came to assist the cause: people like Helen Hayes, Patricia Neal, Frank Capra, Father Daniel Berrigan, William F. Buckley, Jr., Michael Moriarty and Margaret Hamilton, to name just a few.

I remember from the experience of coordinating that event each year that "stars" are generous people who truly like to help when they can; so, I figured, why not approach other popular personalities to help promote the pro-life cause? I did. They didn't. Time after time I contacted important people of great repute. I explained that I needed them to film short public service announcements for use on television that would ask women who are caught in problem pregnancies to choose life. The planned commercials also offered them a telephone number to call for help. Time after time, star after star, the response went something like this: "I really think that what you're doing is wonderful, Father Jim, and I certainly don't condone abortion. I mean, after all, it is killing, right? But, going out front on an issue like this would really get me in a lot of hot water." That from a respected actress in the New York City theater community.

We live, they say, in a free and pluralistic society. All points of view, they parrot, are welcome. But that, I have been finding, is just so much bull. The truth is this: to stand up for life is risky today. "Friends" may well desert you. Jobs may not be so plentiful. I spoke to another actor friend of mine last month. He

25

gets occasional work on daytime soap operas. He, like Joseph of Arimathea, keeps his concerns a secret. He told me that he considers abortion to be a holocaust experience. He said there was no way it isn't murder. I asked him to come with me to a meeting of pro-lifers and speak out. His response was, "I will, but only when I am secure in my career. Speaking on that now could kill my chances with a lot of people in this industry." Experiences like that make you wonder: are we really living in a free society? Or has the fear of not fitting in, of being rejected by others, paralyzed us? Perhaps the "Big Brother is Watching" concept is more of a reality than we know.

Consider this legislative usurpation of our rights and principles: up until now we have been allowed as Catholics to reject abortion in our Catholic hospitals. We were given a choice and we chose to say that no innocent lives would be destroyed in any Catholic institution. Enter the Civil Rights Restoration Act which was debated in Congress. It said that any hospital, Catholic or not, which accepts funding (and all do to some extent) must provide their patients with all medical and surgical services. Translated: the Congress was in the process of eliminating our free choice. They were telling us that to survive financially, Catholic hospitals must offer abortion services. Clearly, we will never do that. If we refuse, they take our funding. Without that funding many of our hospitals cannot survive. Leading us to wonder how free do the pro-choice people really want us to be! Pro-choice means, I'm afraid, their choice, and their choice alone. Is pro-choice really pro-choice? Not on your life!

Question for Reflection

- How free are you in your work environment to speak out in defense of life at every stage?

Our Inconvenient Savior

Back when I was on my high school debate team, we were instructed by our astute coach to be on the lookout for that moment when our opponents would throw away reason and go for the emotional "punch." What they couldn't score with logic they'd replace with heartstring manipulation. Sometimes they could be very convincing. It was our task to remind the judges gently but firmly that as moving as our opposition sounded, they were full of it!

Oftentimes I'm required to debate again, only the issues are more serious now: they are matters of life and death. And once again there exists that key moment when our Planned Parenthood friends and their co-conspirators in the death industry go for the emotional "punch." Failing to convince us that the unborn child isn't really a human person, and ignoring their own 1960s handbook which read, "An abortion kills the life of a baby after it has begun. It is dangerous to your life and health. It may make you sterile so that when you want a child you cannot have it," they use their trump card. They argue that we need legal abortion if only to deal with the many cases of rape or incest, or to eliminate physical danger for an expectant mother, or (they rhetorically ask) how can we ask a woman to carry a child who may be born handicapped? The arguments sound neat and convincing. They really are terribly clever. They play off most people's worst fears for their loved ones. But, you see, they also always leave out the clarifying facts about their "worst case scenarios." They omit, for example, the figures. Of the more than one million abortions performed each year in our nation, fewer than two percent have anything to do with rape, incest, danger to the life of the mother or the possibility of a handicapped child being born. Nor do they ever attempt to address the fundamental question of these crisis pregnancies: does the way in which a child is conceived make the child any less innocent or worthy of the opportunity to be born?

Putting aside the two percent that touch on traumatic considerations, how do we explain the motive behind the other 98 percent of the abortions which occur each year in America? Could it be that the children are inconvenient? These children are "in the way," not part of the plans we make for our lives, guilty of poor timing in arriving on the human scene.

Decisions of convenience. Think about it. Aren't we, all of us, inconvenient and burdensome for others at sometime in our lives? Once we accept the premise that an unborn child can be eliminated because it is inconvenient, we really diminish all of our lives. Think of the elderly: they too can be in the way, they cost a lot to keep healthy and alive, and they're an awful drain on the energies of their younger caretakers. Think of the handicapped and disabled: they certainly never can contribute to our world the way we do, they need special care and consideration, they make us uncomfortable and uneasy because they're "different." Think of the terminally ill: they're going to die anyway and their medical bills can be so high—why not eliminate the problem before it gets out of hand? Let's pull the plug early and save ourselves the needless worry and mess later. Think of the poorest of the poor, the street people, they too are "in the way," they're a frightening sight and they serve no "useful" purpose in society. Why not put them permanently out of our field of vision?

We are all, at times, a source of inconvenience for others. We will all, at times, be a burden for others to carry. And yet, isn't that really part of what being fully human is all about? Isn't being with and for one another tenderly and compassionately, in the good times and the not so good times, part and parcel of the human and Christian vocation?

Each December we celebrate the birth of perhaps the most inconvenient child ever conceived: Jesus, the Lord. His mother, Scripture scholars say, was probably about 16 when she conceived him. She had no visible means of support: no job, little education. The fellow she was engaged to was not the father of the child. The law of the land said that if you conceive a child out of wedlock, the people of the town should take you to the outskirts of the village and stone you to death. If anyone had a right to argue that her pregnancy was "inconvenient" it was Mary, the mother of Jesus. And yet can you imagine how different all of our lives would be had Mary said no instead of yes?

Our God is a God of life and hope and possibility. He is a God who enjoins us to lift and carry the burdens and inconveniences of life with gratitude for the chance to care lovingly for the weakest. The world sometimes seems more inclined to celebrate a god called convenience. To such a god, especially at Christmas, we respond: "Bah! Humbug!"

Question for Reflection

- Which of the reasons suggested here do you find the most convincing in support of life?

Parental Consent

Sometime ago I had dinner with a terrific young couple named John and Lois Donnelly. And before we sat down to eat we spent some time with their children, Lauren and Steven. They are a beautiful family, and they work hard to build this loving community.

I remember when they were considering a new home that John and Lois were really concerned about the needs of their children above all. They investigated the school district they would attend to be sure that it offered quality education. They examined the neighborhood carefully to be sure that their children would meet a wide variety of people. They made sure that the commute to and from work was reasonable so that John could be home early enough to truly enjoy his children and share fully in the responsibility of raising them with Lois. And like many young couples, John and Lois try to create a healthy home for their offspring. They avoid fats, sugars and salt. They exercise and try to stay in shape. They are also very safety conscious and want their home to be a place the children can live in without fear.

Even on a spiritual level John and Lois live out a real concern for their children's welfare. Like many couples they had put church on a back burner after their wedding. But as the children started to arrive, they felt a need to bring a more formal spiritual formation into their lives. They seemed to recognize that the love of God and the support of a faith community could only further enhance their lives. And so, at least initially for their children's sake, they moved back to the Church.

John and Lois are not atypical. Many parents direct their lives and their energies toward the welfare of their children. They move in selfless and giving directions, which radically change their lives. They do it because of the love they feel for this precious gift from God: their children.

Consider now this reality. John and Lois love, nurture, feed, clothe, encourage, counsel, give medical care to and shelter their children. Throughout their children's growth they are consulted and advised. Their permission is sought on every major decision affecting their children by school and society. No doctor will pull a tooth without parental permission. No teacher will take their daughter on a school field trip without parental consent. No nurse will dispense an aspirin without checking with the parents. No store will pierce a child's ear without receiving parental authorization. And these facts all highlight an important parental right: the right to know what is happening in the life of the child they love. Even the Supreme Court recognized the importance of this respect for parents when in 1979 it proclaimed:

"Minors often lack the experience, perspective and judgment to recognize and avoid choices that could be detrimental to them. Parents are entitled to the support of laws designed to aid the discharge of their parental responsibility."

Why then, we might ask, is abortion the one decision about which parents presently have no rights at all? A minor, say age 15, finds out she is pregnant (close to 750,000 teenagers become pregnant every year in America). As the law presently stands, she can go to her teacher; get pro-abortion counseling; be driven to an abortion clinic; have her baby destroyed; in some places have the abortion paid for by the state; and then return home to parents who know nothing of what has transpired.

Oh, there is one catch! If the teenager develops post-abortion complications (and there are plenty of possibilities, like a perforated uterus, a uterine infection, major hemorrhaging, high fever or emotional trauma), then the responsibility for that teenager reverts back to her parents. If the girl is "broken" physically or emotionally by her abortion experience, that's her parents' problem. The same folks who were shut out of the decision to abort are then legally obligated to "pick up the pieces of their child's life."

Pro-abortion spokespersons will often use polls to support the right of people to abort freely. But polls do not help them on the parental consent issue. A 2005 Gallup poll reported 69 percent of those polled believed that parents should be involved in a decision which so profoundly affects their children.

During the early 1960s we would hear awful stories of communist totalitarian antics wherein parents and their children would be encouraged to betray each other. Parents who were unfaithful to the party line could be arrested if their children "fingered them." We all recoiled at that image because we believed that the state simply has no right to come between parents and their children. And yet, presently on abortion, the state is separating parents and their children at what must be seen as one of the most crucial decisions anyone can make: to give life or to take it.

I really admire John and Lois. They are doing everything a parent can to raise healthy and loving children. I hope and pray that they will always be allowed to share a part of each and all of the major moments in their children's lives. How tragic it would be if laws, which supposedly protect "privacy," acted only to separate a child from the best friends she has in the world: devoted parents.

Question for Reflection

- Whose best interest do you think is being served by not having parental consent or parental notification laws in place?

Beauty and the Value of Children

Back in 1984 I had an extraordinary privilege. For a multitude of reasons I was the coach assisting my younger sister Patti in the delivery of her firstborn, Matthew Paul. It was one of the holiest moments of my life. It convinced me, beyond the shadow of a doubt, of the giftedness of human life (the miracle of life takes on an incredible power during the birthing process). When I travel to different parishes to speak about family and respect life concerns, I often mention the incredible experience of witnessing birth. People smile, heads nod, and those who have had a similar experience share their joy. The experience of birth is one of the many ways children offer a special witness to the sanctity of life. Even cynics become believers at the sight of God's little ones. Three very special children remind me of how, in our hearts, we all long to embrace pro-life values. They are Cecilia, Jessica and Lisa.

Cecilia Chican was traveling with her mother, her father and her brother from Detroit to Phoenix. As the plane took off, something went wrong. Losing altitude swiftly, the plane crashed, killing all the passengers on board. Except Cecilia. Miraculously, she was spared. Her survival seemed unexplainable until investigators put the details together. They suggest that as the plane went down, Cecilia's mother covered her daughter's body with her own. In other words, her mother reacted with one of the oldest and most sacred responses: she laid down her life to protect her child. She died so that Cecilia would live. In the Book of Isaiah, the Lord, recognizing the special bonding between mother and child, says, "If a mother would forsake the child of her womb, I, your God, will never desert you." Cecilia's mother lived the selfless love of God. She paid the ultimate price so that her daughter would live. Who of us was not profoundly moved by her sacrifice? In an age when many view children as disposable life, subject to the convenience or inconvenience they present, wasn't it uplifting to witness a mother who chose to put her child above all?

And then there was Jessica McClure, a little girl who made America hold its breath for over 50 hours. "Baby Jessica," fell down an unused well on Oct 14, 1987. The 19-month-old girl was lodged there for a seeming eternity. All prayed, and hoped and wished for her survival. Children were glued to television sets, asking their parents again and again, "Is Jessica out yet? Will she be all right?" Jessica's parents were teenagers. There are many people in our nation who would say that they had no business having a child so early in their lives. But none of that mattered when we saw the picture of Jessica's face. Her smiling eyes and the knowledge of her entombment compelled us to pray constantly for her survival. For over two days we all cared deeply about life. And when they brought her up alive, with cuts and bruises but essentially well, we all cheered and thanked God. Why had we cared so much? How did a small, innocent and unimportant little girl have the power to reduce the most powerful nation in the world to a pool of compassion?

And who can forget Lisa Steinberg? Hearing the news of her abuse sickened us all. How could anyone beat and abuse that beautiful child? Her haunted face looked out from newspapers, seeming to plead for help and comfort. Neighbors, police and social workers did what they could. But it just wasn't enough to save Lisa. Her lingering death made us rethink our obligations to get involved, to stop abuse, to protect our children. Some critics and promoters of death used Lisa as an example. One writer in a major newspaper said that Lisa proved that unwanted pregnancies were better terminated (aborted) than having a child be born, adopted and abused. What incredible ignorance!

Every social study in America indicates that the vast majority of abused children in our country were wanted at conception. They become unwanted after birth. And Lisa was not "adopted," she was stolen. It is a true calumny to lump together the actions of legitimate child care and adoptive service with the way Lisa was obtained by the Steinbergs. Adoption remains what it has always been—a life-giving means of supporting and nurturing our most precious resource. Those who give up their children for adoption and the loving couples who adopt them are heroes for our age.

The stories of Cecilia, Jessica and Lisa were painful and emotionally wrenching. But they had life-producing effects. They caused us to appreciate, just a little more, the beauty and value of our children. And if we take a little more time to hug, to respect and to treasure our young ones, then the tragedies and near tragedies of these three beautiful children will not have been in vain.

Question for Reflection

• Why do you think that the life of an unborn child is not valued as much as a small child's life?

Are You Ready?

Some years ago, I was heading south to a Florida vacation. My traveling companion was another priest. Joe Lukaszewski and I left New York on a flight with one scheduled stop, a quick drop to Atlanta. Then Florida good times would be ours for a week. When we travel, we usually dress in civilian clothes, so no one knew we were priests.

About twenty minutes out of Atlanta something unusual happened. A flight attendant, with her usual charming and gracious manner, invited Joe and me to come up front for a little "discussion." We looked quizzically at each other wondering what was going on.

Once we were a safe distance from other passengers, she told us. The plane, it seemed, was "experiencing some mechanical difficulty." The four of us (she'd selected two other guys as well) were needed to help. "What kind of help?" asked one of the other men. And that's when she proceeded to blow our socks off with the true nature of the situation. The plane's wings, we were told, have flaps that are lowered at landing time. The flaps slow the plane down to a stoppable speed. Well, the flaps are controlled by a hydraulic system. And, you guessed it, the hydraulic system was "not functioning." In other words, instead of coming in at a normal speed, we were going to land at a speed that was significantly faster. This she told us, might well result in the loss of tires and landing gear once we hit the runway. More simply—she told us we should expect to make an "emergency landing." One of the other fellows cut to the heart of it: "Are you saying we're going to crash-land?" The flight attendant, trained in the language of illusion, responded, "We prefer the term emergency landing." Call it what you will—I was scared.

The attendant had shared this news with us because she required our help for emergency evacuation. One fellow was to body block the aisle to help discourage panic once we "landed."

Another was to assist people out the door. My friend Joe was to push the door handle that would, in turn, open the door and release a slide for passengers to use to exit. And my job? I had the best of all. Once we landed and the door was open, I was to go down the slide first and move away from the plane. In anticipation of fire or smoke, I was to yell "over here" to confused or disoriented passengers, so they would move away from the endangered plane.

After we received all these instructions, the other passengers were informed of our dilemma. You never heard a less noisy airplane. No one spoke; the silence seemed to suggest even the absence of breathing. My friend Joe looked positively green. As we came in for the attempt at landing, some people prayed, others cried, most just did as they were told—placing their heads between their legs to blunt the effects of our touchdown without tires.

We made it. Oh, it was rough, a few tires went, but we were fine. A few people did leave swearing "never to fly again." A few people, I suspect, spent considerable time in the airport rest rooms, but we made it.

About a week after the Atlanta landing, I started to put the whole thing into some perspective. I started to play the "what ifs." Suppose we hadn't made it? And you find yourself wondering: Is the fighting we do with each other worth it? Are the cruel things we say really so necessary? Are the ambitions we harbor so important? Are the grudges we hold logical? Are the opportunities we miss to say "I love you" so unimportant? Are the good deeds we always meant to do so easily excused and deferred?

No one really believes that death lives around the corner. And so we go on as if time on this planet is endless. That's very human and also very stupid. My air trip to Florida had a happy ending. But it might just as easily have been the whole shooting match. And the time to bring the love, the goodness, the charity, the forgiving and the hoped-for togetherness is now.

Question for Reflection

- What event has helped you put life into a proper perspective?

Miracle

As I drive along in my car, I often listen to popular music. Usually it's simply background melody. But sometimes I listen to the words. One day I heard a Whitney Houston hit called "Miracle." It's a love song—but a love song with a difference. The singer is telling us that she chose to turn her back on love. She chose to end the "miracle" which is life. And, she tells us, nothing is worth that choice. The song is a warning. It encourages the listener to choose wisely. And it reminds us that when we make a selfish choice, we compromise not only the dignity of our unborn child, but our own dignity as well.

Whitney Houston's song could well be the theme song for any person who's ever experienced an abortion. She talks about the dangers of "throwing it all away." And "it" is the new life, the miracle which is her baby. The question is often asked: Is it a choice or is it a baby? And Whitney Houston clearly tells us: it's both. The choice is real, but so are the painful consequences.

Often we speak about the child as abortion's victim, and indeed, the baby is the greatest victim. But we sometimes forget abortion's other victim. And that person is the mother who knows that where there was once life and possibility, there's now only great emptiness, a pervading sadness and hurt.

And it doesn't just affect women. Many times I've met men who encouraged or promoted an abortion for their wives or girlfriends. Some, for a while, excused themselves by saying: "It was her choice, her decision," but they know in their hearts the truth of it all. And they realize that in encouraging abortion they were participants in a disastrous choice.

There is a wonderful book on the hurts and pain suffered by those who choose to abort their babies. It's called *A Path to Hope* and should greatly aid the wounded "other victims" of abortion. Written by John Dillon, who has had broad experience in healing these hurts, *A Path to Hope* is important reading for ministers and counselors, as well as friends and family of those who have experienced abortion. The author compassionately describes a condition called post-abortion syndrome (P.A.S.). He speaks with tenderness and mercy of the woman who has had an abortion and tells us that the surviving victim of abortion often suffers from the following symptoms:

Low self-esteem. It's hard for a person who chooses abortion to feel good about herself. Nice people, she believes, don't do things like this. Good people don't destroy life. And so, she reasons, "I must not be good. I must have little value as a human being." She sees her value in severely diminished terms.

Guilt. The person who aborts realizes that values and standards have been betrayed. No one is raised to believe that abortion is a good thing. We all know it destroys innocent life. The aborted woman also recognizes that she's turned her back on life-affirming values. She doesn't have to be a very religious person to imagine that God is severely displeased with her actions. And in fact, sometimes the woman who experiences abortion is harder on herself than God would ever be. I've known women who said, "I know God is merciful. It's me who can't accept His forgiveness."

Depression. This can be chronic or acute. And, Dillon tells us, it reflects itself in a variety of ways. Mood swings, crying, an inability to make decisions, disinterest in life, listlessness, and a lack of physical energy are some of the telltale signs of P.A.S.

Suicidal thoughts. The mixture of diminished self-esteem, guilt and depression can be deadly. They can make a person feel that hope is impossible. And the absence of hope can lead a person to the desire to quell life's pain. Suicide can seem to be a way to make the pain disappear.

Broken relationships. Few people continue to date the person with whom they conceived their now aborted child. And for married persons who choose abortion, the dysfunction can be especially severe. It's common to blame one another for the decision to abort, or to resent the lack of firmness in trying to prevent the abortion from happening. And every time the two parents look into each other's eyes, they are reminded that together they have created a life now ended.

Other signs of P.A.S. include nightmares, sleeplessness, flashbacks to the abortion, anger, drug or alcohol abuse, sexual promiscuity and dysfunction, phobias, compulsive disorders and an inability to relate comfortably to other children.

A Path to Hope not only discusses these P.A.S. symptoms, but outlines a way out of the pain. This book is a beacon of light breaking through what can be incredible darkness. I cannot recommend it highly enough.

(To get a copy of *A Path to Hope* by John Dillon, go to www.catholicbookpublishing.com.)

Question for Reflection

- Abortion carries many aftereffects in its wake in the life of the mother. Yet some people are anxious that women considering abortions not be told about these possibilities. Consider this fact. Why should this be? Is this consistent with a patient's right to know all the pros and cons of any other type of surgery?

Real Life

Let me describe the situation. A newly married pregnant mother receives a call that her young husband has been killed in a car accident. She is devastated that she will have to raise the unborn child alone. She is without the financial means to do that. Her husband, while much loved, left no money behind. The mother realizes that she will have to find a job and worries about who will care for her child while she's gone. She has yet to finish school and has no discernible job skills. Her situation does not look promising.

There are counselors in family planning clinics across the nation who would find these circumstances ripe for abortion. They would warn this pregnant mother that her odds of juggling school, job, day care and the successful raising of her child are almost impossible. They would tell her that the most sensible thing to do is to abort the child and move on with schooling and career without the "burden" of a poorly-timed pregnancy.

And if they were successful at convincing that mother to abort, they would have been destroying a past occupant of the White House — because the story above is his story. His life began with a challenging pregnancy. His Dad did die before he was born. His mother Virginia was poor, without a formal education, jobless and without job skills. When she decided to go to New Orleans and secure the education needed to be a nurse, she had to leave baby Bill with his grandparents for over two years until she could get a degree. Money was always tight, and having this child seriously limited Virginia Clinton's life.

So when I see a man like Bill Clinton promote abortion in our land and export it to other lands, I find myself wondering: Doesn't he see the contradiction? Doesn't Mr. Clinton recognize that 98 percent of American abortions are performed (according to the *New York Times*) for "reasons of social convenience"? And doesn't he see that his own development in the womb was also "socially inconvenient"?

Seeing the reality of abortion means that we have to open our eyes wide to the reality of its horror. So, for example, most African-American members of the United States Congress support abortion. And most of these representatives would argue that abortion allows black women the freedom to achieve economic benefit by not saddling them with "unwanted children." But consider this reality: we've aborted 31 million children since *Roe v. Wade*. African Americans make up less than 20 percent of our population. But over one-third of the abortions performed in America are done to black babies. In other words, we're destroying black children at numbers that far exceed their white counterparts. So that when black congresspersons vote to promote abortion, they help to advance a real black genocide. How is it helping the African-American community to kill its own children? If the problem is poverty, then let's work to eradicate that injustice. But to kill the future, where is the logic in that?

I don't think Bill Clinton connects his own story to the abortions he now promotes. I don't think that black leaders understand that "abortion rights" are destroying future generations of kids who deserve to live. I don't think most of us understand the extent of the savagery which is abortion. But we should. This is, after all, real life.

Question for Reflection

- Can you think of other people besides Bill Clinton—either well-known people or known to you personally—that were born into a situation that might have been considered ripe circumstances for abortion? Do you think that these people would rather not have been born? What about the world: Would the world have been better or worse off without them?

Deadly Silence

The New York State Right to Life Committee recently asked me to give a talk on the subject of working with clergy. The feeling of the committee was that many clergy are unwilling or unable to become involved in the battle against abortion. Their invitation echoed a report from the National Conference of Catholic Bishops. At a recent meeting of pro-life directors, the results of a national survey indicated that priests do tend to be relatively silent and uninvolved on this issue. The conference reported that in no way were most priests supportive of abortion. Just the opposite was true. They detest the taking of pre-born life. But the study also indicated that many priests said they just had no idea how to work this explosive subject into the context of their preaching.

I had a personal experience some years ago that spoke to the reticence of my brother priests. I was out for dinner with a dear friend (a priest) who I know is definitely pro-life. I complained about the lack of pro-life preaching, and he started to look uncomfortable. So I asked him the obvious question: "How often would you give a homily on abortion?" He sheepishly admitted that he had never delivered a sermon on the subject. He said he was silent because "it's so controversial, and people might get upset or angry. It's such a political football." My friend was right. The subject is difficult and controversial. People do feel deeply on abortion. Some will love you for talking about it. Others will resent the topic. Some may even get up and leave the church to avoid the subject. But admitting all that. I'm not sure that we, as clergy, really have much of a choice. We don't truly have the freedom to remain silent in the face of evil.

I find myself deeply drawn to books about the Second World War, and particularly intrigued by those that examine the Catholic Church in Germany during the reign of national socialism. Bishops and priests clearly understood the darkness that was Nazism. Many took the risk and rose to the pulpit to denounce it. Most, however, remained quiet. They didn't actively support Hitler; they just thought it best to be silent in their opposition. Some did speak up strongly and paid a heavy price. Not a few died for their courage.

I think the comparison holds. We live in a society that treats life as a disposable commodity. Over 30 million lives have already been lost to abortion. I know no priest who considers abortion a good thing. The universal Church decries it as a "grave sin." The teaching of the Church is unambiguous. So why, then, are we silent?

Add to all this the reality of choice. A lot of people perceive the Church as monolithic on abortion. They expect that most Catholics oppose it. But in fact, among all religious groups in America, no group chooses to abort its children at a higher rate than Catholics. More than Jews. More than Protestants. More than those with no religion at all. Catholics are the highest aborters in America. Again, how can we be silent?

Then there's the issue of politics. Many clergy fear that speaking about abortion somehow involves them in illegal political activity. Some fear that the Church's tax exempt status may be compromised by speaking out. This is untrue. We are permitted by law to speak about moral issues and legislation from the pulpit. We are not permitted to endorse particular candidates. And politics, whether we like it or not, is the means by which governments implement moral choices. Opposing apartheid involves politics. Opposing the contras involved politics. Bringing calm to Bosnia involved politics. Stopping slavery involved politics. Politics and political issues need to be addressed. And where politics directly compromises our moral principles, we are obliged to speak out.

An example comes to mind. An attempt to include abortion funding in national health policy would force all of us to pay for other people's abortions, millions of them. To remain silent in the face of such legislation is to endorse the use of our tax dollars to terminate pre-born children. Silence, in such a case, aids the oppressor. It cooperates with evil. It makes us co-conspirators of the abortion holocaust.

I am not naive. I do not believe that preaching alone can end the tragedy of abortion. But in an age where the law will not protect unborn children, winning over the hearts and minds of our people becomes even more clearly a matter of life and death.

Question for Reflection

- How can you help to have more preaching on abortion?

Part II

More of Love

Sex Respect

The Church often takes a bad rap about sex. People believe that Catholics see sex as dirty, as wrong, as sinful. We don't. We believe sex is beautiful, good and even holy. It's just a question of where you share it and what your motive is for giving one of the deepest parts of yourself to another person. The place to do it is in marriage. The reason to do it is real love.

For many years experts—psychologists and sociologists—have been grappling with the question: why do teenagers and young adults want sex? The obvious answer is that sex feels good. But that's way off the mark. There are, experts say, many non-sexual motives for why we desire sex. And coming to terms with why we want something can give us the courage to choose a better way of living.

In every report and study I've seen, these are the main reasons why we chase sex:

1. *Self-esteem.* We lack it. We want it. And we mistakenly believe that if we have sex we'll feel better about ourselves. Our teenage and young adult years can be filled with insecurity, confusion and sometimes emotional chaos. We'll grab at anything that promises to make us like ourselves better. The catch is sex won't do much to enhance our self-esteem, and probably will damage it—because self-esteem isn't based only on what we do (e.g., sex), but on who we are.

2. *Peer pressure.* None of us wants to be left out. If everybody is doing it, it's natural to want to join the crowd. The "crowd" is smaller than we think. Polling information confirms that about 32 percent of teenagers have sex before they graduate. That's bad news, but it sure doesn't represent a majority. Author Karen Catchpole writes that people who don't have sex may think they are "weird, defective, undersexed . . . not cool." Well, if that's what virgins are, then there are a lot of us there. Be relieved, we're not alone.

3. *I need love.* The culture in which we live has made some terrible equations. They've tried to convince us that sex equals love. It doesn't. In fact, in test studies of that 32 percent who have had sex, their response to the experience placed "love" way down the list of feelings they had after sex. Above it were "foolish," "used," "manipulated," "bad" and "regretful." And anyone who says that we prove our love by having sex is snowing you. Love doesn't have to be "proved." Love is a free gift, not one we have to pressure another into putting out.

4. *Rebellion.* From day one most of us have to answer to people in charge. Parents, teachers, coaches, older brothers and sisters, the Church, the principal. For many years we kind of accept the authorities who run our lives. But, inevitably, it happens. We decide to blow away the people in charge. One of the ways we do that is by rejecting their values and their rules. We stop going to Church. We try drinking and sometimes even drugs. We experiment with sex. These are ways in which we assert our independence. Don't mistake any of these actions for maturity or responsible freedom. They're adolescent responses to perceived frustrations. They're inappropriate reactions. The way we should respond to a need for greater freedom is to negotiate and reason with the authorities in our lives.

5. *Escape.* Our homes are not like Bill Cosby's. We don't have it all together. Conflict, division and unhappiness reign in many homes. People pick and nag. Celebrating the negative is how many parents respond to pressure. Young persons often crave escape from unhappy homes. One escape hatch that can promise temporary relief is sex. For just a few hours, at least, we think we can escape the hostile world we live in. But like most artificial escapes, the sexual release just puts us back where we started.

When I was a junior in high school my dearest friend died of cancer. She was a classmate and a tremendous person. For months after her death I did some incredibly stupid things,

things I'd rather forget. Finally, after many mistakes, someone, at long last, confronted me, "Jim, don't you think you should deal with Chris' death instead of doing all these asinine things?"

That question hit me like a cold bucket of water in the face. I was avoiding the "why" of my behavior. And unless we know the why, we can never get out from under.

That's true of sex, too. We've got lots of motives for why we do what we do. And understanding our motives can give us the freedom to choose a better way.

Question for Reflection

• Which of the five reasons highlighted here do you consider the most relevant and why?

Coming Clean

You never forget your first car. I remember every detail about mine. It was a Chevrolet Nova, sky blue and beautiful. I couldn't afford it without some financial help from my parents. They were glad to pitch in, their only condition for assistance was that I "drive carefully!" Once, that warning was fine, but it became a common chorus every time I left the house. How foolish I thought they were. Why worry? Clearly, Nova and I were destined for a long and wonderful relationship, right? Wrong. Not fully two months after I got the car, disaster struck. I was heading home far too late from a long and exhausting high school reunion. I remember thinking: it would be nice just to close my eyes and rest for a second (a dumb idea when you're driving at 40 miles an hour). My next memory was seeing my car wrapped around another car. Nobody, thank God, was hurt. But poor Nova was history.

It took me a good day or so to call home from college. My mother was understandably upset. She told me that my father was away on business and suggested I call him with the news. "That won't be necessary," I said. "Why is that?" she asked. "Well, I'm not telling Dad about the accident." I don't remember exactly what my mother said in response, but the gist of it was: it's going to be kind of hard to explain the missing car over the next few years.

She was right. I had to come clean. I had to tell him. The next few days were awful. I worried constantly. I was sure my father would lose it. Certain that he'd chew me out. Convinced that he'd never help me again. I felt like a frightened, stupid fool. Three days after the conversation with my mother, with a knot in my stomach, sweaty palms and a huge tension headache, I called my father. Speaking quickly, I broke the news. Long pause. Dad responds, "Was anyone hurt?" "No." "All right, all right, relax, we'll talk about it when I get home." That was it. No screaming, no put-down, no "How could you be so stupid?" Just concern coupled with the sound of relief that no one had been hurt.

Too often we sell our parents short. We judge their limitations, and evaluate their coping abilities without giving them a real chance. Another example comes to mind. I had a visit one day from a young couple in the parish who I knew had been dating for about a year. When they came to see me, I could tell that something was making them incredibly tense. Finally, Valerie broke the news: "Father Jim, we're pregnant." I was happy for their expected child, if not thrilled with the way the baby occurred, but there were other challenges ahead. "Look, Father, Kevin and I love each other and we believe that it is wrong to get rid of the baby." I, obviously, agreed. "But Father, my parents don't even know that we've been fooling around; and if they find out that not only were we having sex, but that I'm pregnant, they'll kill me."

This was not the first time I'd heard about "parents who'd never understand." In most high schools I visit, the very first reason students give for why they'd have to abort is the fear of telling their parents the truth. Parents become the fall guys in this difficult situation.

I proposed to Valerie a possible solution for breaking the news. I would go with them. She agreed, and later that night we arrived at her parents' home. Her father was very warm and welcoming. At this point, he had no idea what the nice priest was doing in his home. But in the next half hour the tone of our visit would change.

True to Valerie's predictions, her father went crazy when faced with this unexpected news. He yelled, he cursed and he called her a slut. He promised to throw her out of the house. Meanwhile, her mother cried, and her boyfriend Kevin just kept quite.

After many hours of hysteria, we called it a night. Valerie's dad stayed angry for about a month. He did not throw her out of the house. He stopped being angry, and then, gradually, he came around. He started to drive Valerie to the doctor, he nagged her about eating right, and he complained about her smoking, because "it would hurt the kid."

I have a final, perduring recollection about this family. When little Vanessa was born, I had the privilege of baptizing her. And when the christening was over, I stood at the back door of the church to say good-bye. The person who was lovingly cradling this beautiful baby in his arms was grandpa. His eyes were bright with gentleness and tenderness. For beyond the anger and the confusion and the pain of seeing his daughter make a mistake, he was what all parents strive to be: a good, caring and compassionate friend.

Friends like these should be given a chance. They deserve the risk of our trust, our honesty and our love.

We need to come clean with our parents. They're worth it!

Questions for Reflection

- Teenagers: Does Valerie's and Keven's situation and the way it worked out ring true to you? Why? Why not?

- Parents: Put yourself in Valerie's parents' place. Would you be able to rise to the occasion—support them in their choice for life?

Parents

I think that Matthew Broderick is a terrific actor. You will remember him in movies like *War Games, Ferris Bueller's Day Off* and *Project X*.

In one of his first films, *Max Duggan Returns*, he played a pretty normal teenager in a single-parent home. He enjoys a good relationship with his mom. They talk; they laugh, and they're honest with each other. My favorite scene, though, deals with the influence of peer pressure on our parental relationships. Matthew's mother is driving him to school. Normally, he would kiss her good-bye as he left the car.

But on this particular day she pulls up to a place outside the school where several of his friends are hanging out. Absurdly, he tries to shake his mother's hand to say good-bye. He doesn't want to look affectionate in front of his friends, at least toward his mom. His mother, beautifully played by Marsha Mason, pulls him right back in the car.

She short-circuits his speedy departure to tell him that expressing love shouldn't end just because "the jerks are watching." It's a good lesson for Matthew and a timely one for all of us too.

These days are probably a good time to reflect on the relationships we have (or don't have) with our parents. Imagine someone giving us a monumental important responsibility for which you had little or no training. And the commitment isn't for a day, or a week, or a month, but for a lifetime. That's the situation for most parents. They don't go to school to learn how to do it right. They learn by doing. Now that means, at times, they will botch it badly; but at least they try.

As their children, we start out as totally dependent. We count on our parents for food, for shelter, for clothing, for laughter, and for comfort in sharing our fears. We especially count on them for love. Then something strange happens to us.

We seem, for a few years, to outgrow the need for our parents. We begin to distance ourselves from them at the very time in our lives when we are most insecure, most in need of support, most vulnerable, and weakest in our self-esteem.

Our teenage years are, all experts agree, a time of transition and a period of awkward and lurching growth. We need stability and loyalty; at the same time we seem to run most quickly from it. Suddenly the people who helped to bring us to this age are shunted aside and seen as irrelevant, or embarrassing, or ignorant of the world. Leaving them out is definitely a mistake. They have an insight, from being with us from the beginning, that no one else can have. They've learned, often from making mistakes, what we need and who we are. Shutting them out is a senseless waste.

All of it reminds me of my own high school years. I grew up being pretty open about expressing affection. Small children have a freedom about loving that isn't tainted by fear of what peers will think. And then, as adolescence took hold, I remember backing off from expressing love to my parents, especially my father. It simply wasn't macho or cool to kiss your dad. People (I thought) would look down on that.

Well, one day my dad and I were watching the Superbowl together. I was about 16. And the hero of the Superbowl-winning Jets was Joe Namath. Now, remember that "Broadway Joe" was reputed to be a lady killer. He was a true masculine stereotype. He was what everyone wants to be. Well, he wins the big one and goes back to the locker room to celebrate. All of his teammates are busy talking to reporters and popping champagne.

Joe, the star quarterback, doesn't. Instead, he wanders over to a corner of the room and literally picks up and hugs this little greyhaired man; then he plants a kiss on the man: his dad. In this moment of supreme joy, with the whole world watching, he wasn't afraid to demonstrate his gratitude and love to someone he treasured. I remember thinking, back in 1969, that if it's okay for Joe Namath, why should I be treating my father like a stranger?

From that time on, I have never missed the opportunity to show my dad and mom that I care. And, you know, beyond the first few times of expressing affection again, it really wasn't so hard to do.

Question for Reflection

* What makes it hard for you to show affection to your family members?

Interfaith Marriage

Wherein a generation ago only ten percent of Catholics selected a partner who was not Catholic, now the percentage has jumped to 32 percent. And the increase is fraught with difficulties that couples will need to confront early in their engaged and dating relationships.

It is no accident that more interfaith couples end their relationships in divorce than those marrying a person of the same faith. It takes a couple willing to confront a variety of pitfalls and differences to make interfaith marriage work. In the sections below, I will attempt to outline some of the challenges, and possible solutions, to the interfaith marriage issue:

1. *Love doesn't conquer all.* Many interfaith couples know that there are serious differences between their two faiths. They recognize that the differences aren't going to go away, but they sincerely believe that love offers a surefire balm for every potential problem. It doesn't. The differences must be dealt with early and openly. The ostrich route is no solution. Love is a wonderful thing, but it cannot be used to replace dialogue and discernment.

2. *"Aren't we really all the same, anyway?"* Some people become ecumenical like nobody's business when they meet and fall in love with a person of another faith. They ignore the religious, the cultural and the traditional hurdles in favor of a view of all religions as "essentially the same." To deny our differences is naive at best. We are the products of highly varied theological backgrounds and points of view. We were immersed in these beliefs at a tender and formative age. We are not likely to sweep away our long-held beliefs and traditions too easily. Nor should we. When we fall in love with someone, we love all that the person is, and we need to recognize that our Catholic, or Jewish, or Protestant upbringing helped to shape the person we love into that particular human being. To

erase the differences or make believe that they don't exist is to deny a part of who and what we are.

3. *Dispensations matter.* We went through a time when couples living together would argue that marriage is "just a piece of paper, a legality." There is a similar tendency towards Church dispensations as well. To marry a person of another faith, the Catholic partner needs to sign a dispensation. This promise states that because his Catholic faith means so much to him, he will do all in his power to have their children baptized and reared as Roman Catholics.

A second dispensation is filled out if the couple wishes to be married outside of a Catholic church. A Catholic/Protestant couple may be married in the church of either family. A Catholic/Jewish couple may celebrate their wedding in a Catholic church; in a Jewish synagogue; or in a neutral setting (e.g., an interfaith chapel, a catering hall).

The dispensation is a controversial item. Some view it as a way of exerting control over the religious destiny of children. It isn't meant to be a control issue at all. When we celebrate a Baptism, we are fundamentally saying two things. First, that we want our child to know Jesus. We are saying that our child's life would be infinitely poorer if he were to go through life without understanding the joy, the compassion, the forgiveness, the friendship and the life-saving goodness of a relationship with Christ. We are also saying that we want our child to belong to a community of faith. We want our children to have a particular direction and sense of identity. We want for our children, wherever they go in life, to know that they have a home in the Catholic Church.

Like the purposes of Baptism, the dispensation is a way of committing our children to a particular religious direction. It doesn't preclude the full knowledge of the non-Catholic spouse's faith. It is just saying that life is filled with particular choices, one of which is, "What faith will I learn and try to live?"

Some argue that a child should be directed to no particular faith but be made aware of all faiths and decide on a particular faith in adulthood. That sounds good but it's not very practical. Any parent who has tried to teach even one faith well knows that it's often an overwhelming task. To offer your child a religious smorgasbord is much harder to accomplish than couples might realize.

Another compromise practiced by some couples is the notion of bypassing the religion of both husband and wife and raising the child in a neutral "third religion." While that might seem "politic," it is really ignoring the richness of two already developed faiths in favor of a third, about which nothing is known. It tends to further separate families already grappling with religious differences. Instead of two divisions we now have three.

Some couples, in an attempt to bypass the critical impact of a dispensation, will dismiss it as "just one more Church rule." Many sign the promise intending to ignore its conditions. Sadly, even some priests attempt to minimize the requirements of the dispensation. Filled with a desire to be "nice guys," priests can water down the meaning of the promise.

That's really a dishonest disservice to the engaged couple. A promise is what we have always known it to be: the giving of our word. We place our very lives in the words we promise. And if our words are untrue, so are we.

You may recall in the powerful drama, *A Man for All Seasons*, that St. Thomas More is encouraged by his daughter Lady Margaret to tell King Henry VIII what he wants to hear. More is advised by his daughter that he should keep in his heart his true beliefs, while telling the king that he agrees with him. St. Thomas responds by saying, "When a man takes an oath, Meg, he's holding his own self in his own hands." We have only our word. When a man stands beside a woman before the altar of God and promises "to love and honor you all the days of my life," he is giving his word, he is giving his promise. A wife is impelled to trust and believe. So, too, the Church trusts and longs to believe in the sincerity of the Catholic who seeks a dispensation to marry a person of another faith. Please, do not promise what you will not try to live.

4. *Conversion is between God and you.* To "streamline" religious differences, people sometimes encourage their intended to convert. It's thought that this will eliminate any conflicts or problems. But that's like deciding what someone's relationship with God will be, without asking God what he thinks. Conversion is a spiritual journey. It isn't a political decision to achieve peace at any price. We can't legislate a religious belief for our spouse. The person we love must be called, not pressured, into embracing a particular faith. If freely chosen, faith can be a wonderful gift. If force-fed, it can be an uncomfortable albatross of little meaning or purpose.

5. *Love and respect your parents, but marry your spouse.* It has always been the teaching of our Church that the primary relationship in marriage must be between a husband and wife. No one and no thing must get in the way of that bonding. Oftentimes, with the best of intentions, our parents attempt to play a major role in the issues that an engaged couple must face within interfaith marriage. Our parents, who may not have been the most devout Catholics, or the most devout Protestants, become terribly interested in religion when it looks like their grandchild isn't going to be of the same faith. We can become very territorial about our religion when we sense an alien presence. The engaged couple must make whatever decisions need to be made with a deep sense of respect for their parents. But the ultimate decision must be their own.

Interfaith marriage is becoming much more commonplace

and acceptable. It is, however, still no easy hurdle. It requires much dialogue and honesty between the engaged. It can, with openness, even become an advantage. Most Catholics don't dialogue much about the role of religion in marriage. They presume that it will play a role, but leave that role undefined. Interfaith couples don't have that luxury, they must talk about it and use their hearts and minds to make serious concrete decisions. In this, interfaith couples are experiencing, perhaps, their first "working through" of a marital challenge. Interfaith marriage can work, but only with a powerful sense of devotion, mutual respect, dialogue and sensitivity.

Question for Reflection

- Can you give an example of an interfaith marriage that has successfully negotiated the religion aspect?

Family Perspective

In view of some of the more significant challenges facing contemporary families, let me attempt here to suggest several possible solutions to the crises we face.

See family as domestic Church. We need to see the people in our family as sacred. There is a need to diminish the cold and, at times, boiling warfare which fills our homes. When people come to me in confession, I often confront family wars through the penance I ask. I request that for one solid week they should say only what is positive, supportive and affirming to family members. They are asked to use the gift of speech to build up, not tear down. This would (if followed) eliminate cursing, nagging, swearing, put-downs, envy, sarcasm and rudeness within our homes.

Repudiation of all violence. Hitting, slapping, kicking another member of the family is a sickness. The person who hits a family member needs help. But he or she does not deserve or require the cooperation of martyrs. At the first sock in the jaw, the sane spouse should draw the line. Putting up with domestic violence is almost as disturbing as committing such violence. Do not cooperate with a person's illness by laying down and playing doormat. Challenge the oppressor to get help or get out.

Divorced men—shame on you! A failed marriage is not license to deprive your wife and children of their financial and emotional support. It is tragic that men continue to punish their families following a divorce by failing to pay court-ordered support or being unwilling to visit the children they helped to create. The reality of poverty among divorced women with children is a striking indictment of men's self-centeredness. Failing to pay child support is another form of child abuse. The wounds are social, but they hurt as surely as if a father kicked his child in the stomach.

Alcohol and drug abuse require help. No one in our family should ever be blamed for being an alcoholic or drug abuser. Alcoholism and related abuse is a disease. Disease left unchecked destroys family life. We cannot blame someone for being ill; we can judge them harshly for failing to seek help.

Sexism in the kitchen. Women are no longer limited to life around the home. They work as long and as hard as men do (and often for less money). It is insensitive in the extreme to expect a woman to work all day outside the home and then perform around the home as if the house was her only concern. Shopping, cleaning, cooking, doing laundry, scrubbing bathrooms and changing diapers are not properly male or female jobs. They are simply necessary for domestic order. If both parents work, these tasks should be evenly shared.

Child abuse is never acceptable. There are two kinds of illnesses in a home scorched by child abuse. The first sickness involves the person who lashes out at his child because internal peace is absent. The second illness rests with the second parent who allows such abuse to continue. The scars of child abuse last a lifetime. They are everyone's concern.

Poverty is everyone's problem. The impoverished single-parent family living in the next village will, sooner or later, directly impact on me and my family. We are naive to believe that we can live in a fortress of safety from the realities of poverty and the resulting despair, criminal activity, drug incidence, and the fostering of racial and ethnic hatreds. Helping the poor to achieve a greater spirit of dignity is the concern of every citizen. The growing rate of infant mortality among the poor is a serious crisis which should shame us and compel us to do more.

Divorce—a painful reality. Divorce used to be a closeted reality in "nice" Catholic families. It is no secret anymore. We need, in each parish, to establish support groups to nourish those whose lives have come undone.

Preventing divorce. There are few, if any, surefire methods of preventing divorce. But certainly a couple's attitudes toward marriage need to be carefully developed before any wedding takes place. Beyond romance, passion and the big wedding lies the real world. And engaged couples need to ask themselves: am I entering marriage for the long distance, or am I really only "giving it a try"?

The glue. I was blessed to work in a program called Retrouvaille (Rediscovery). It is a weekend and follow-up experience for couples in marital crisis. It has been very successful in healing marriages that seemed to be over. Retrouvaille contains no miracle cure, no "quick fix." It simply teaches couples the fundamentals of effective communication, forgiveness and love. It impacts not only on marital discord but on the basic problems facing families in America today. The glue for healing our wounded families is the same principle we try to use in Respect Life programs. All life has its source in God. God gives life. All life is ultimately returning to God. Our beginning and our end is Him. That fact makes life, and wives, and husbands, and children, and families sacred. If we really believed in the holiness of each created person our families would be in much healthier shape. But so long as the sacred is what we do in Church, and not what we live at home, our families will continue to suffer without hope.

(If you would like more information on the state of the American family and how we can respond to the problems of Christian family life, you might want to secure a copy of the document, *A Family Perspective in Church and Society* (published in 1988 and 1998 by the U.S. Conference of Catholic Bishops). It can be obtained from USCCB Publishing (www.usccbpublishing.org).

Question for Reflection

- How has one of the crises mentioned affected your loved ones?

Remembering Michael

Michael was my cousin. We were born a year apart. And as I have two sisters, he was—for a time—like a brother to me. Being a year older made him feel protective of me. We lived in Brooklyn, and Michael was an intuitive street kid. He had smarts about real life I couldn't even begin to have. Michael was cool. He knew the deal. I admired him. He was also talented. Not in an academic way, but with an ability to read people. He was sensitive; he was funny; he could be very kind; he was handsome; and he was charming. He could get you to believe that whatever he said was the absolute truth. Even if it was all bull.

Somewhere, during high school I think, Michael and I started to head down different roads. He got involved with a world that was foreign to me. He drank a lot; he did drugs a lot; he fooled around a lot. And sometimes he got burnt.

His parents, his teachers and some of his friends would try to challenge him to pull it all together. But he was an unbelievable con-man. He would look you in the eyes; tell you that drugs and alcohol were the worst; swear he was finished with them; get you to smile supportively; and be stoned the next day.

This went on for years. And the truth is that we all knew that he was full of it. We wanted to believe in him enough that we accepted what we should have rejected. I can remember many occasions when I'd be sitting with Mike and asking him about how his "problem" was coming. And he would, as always, assure me that things had been low, but now he was really on the right track. One time, to confirm the ruse, he even gave me some of the pills he'd been addicted to. "Throw them out," he said. "I wanna be clean again." I bought the act only to find out that what he'd given me was only a fraction of what he had. And, you know, deep down I always knew he was lying. But it's so hard to say that. It's so difficult to look at someone you love, listen to their stories and to blow them out of the water by telling them that you're not buying a word of it. Maybe sometimes I wanted to keep

Michael's love and friendship more than I needed to expose the unspoken truth.

One day, two years ago, the lies caught up with Michael. He got up in the middle of the night and took into his body more than it could handle. He overdosed, and died within hours.

His death devastated us all. We should have seen it coming, but I guess we denied the inevitable. Our feelings during the wake and funeral were all jumbled. We were angry about drugs; we were angry with Michael; we were angry with God; and if we were really honest, we'd have to admit we were most angry with ourselves. Because, deep down, we knew that we could have done more.

During the Christmas season our families get together to celebrate a lot of wonderful values. But sometimes the holidays also give us opportunities we miss. We've got a chance to be with people we love. Partying with them, eating with them, going to church with them, giving gifts to them, are all important and good; but we also need to use our times together to tell each other the truth—even truths that make us uncomfortable or angry.

For some strange reason, the holidays reawaken our memories. And my memories are often of Michael. I miss him. I loved him, and I wish I had loved him enough to say "stop."

Whatever the person you love is doing—drugs, drinking, sex, lying, cheating, stealing, or putting people down—it's a true sign of caring to confront and to challenge. Real friends aren't the ones who tell us "yes, yes, yes." Our truest friends may have to say no. And "no" is, after all, a love word too.

Questions for Reflection

- Who, in your life, have you had to confront in love?
- Who needs to be confronted?

Betsy's Love

So often it's easy to complain about young people—about their values, about their choices. About the mistakes they make. Sometimes, when adults complain, you get a sense that we've forgotten our own youth. Forgotten the free-spirited errors we also made on the path of life. Hindsight, of course, makes us selectively forget that sometimes we made a mess of it too.

Truth is, I suspect, that some young people are confused about their values; and many do make horrendous mistakes about love, and sex, and commitment. But many others are on the right path. They know who they are; they choose wisely; and they understand love and commitment with a wisdom well beyond their chronological years. Such a person was Betsy Toy.

I first met Betsy when she was fifteen. Even then she was a vibrant and dynamic personality: quick-witted and pretty, full of life and freely willing to tell you what she thought. Raised in a very Catholic family, she was, nonetheless, well able to recognize the good and the less good in a Church she attended regularly. Like most people in high school she went through the usual "crushes." But deep inside I think Betsy always knew that true love was a precious commodity, something rare and true. Something you have to look for carefully.

In her later teens, Betsy came to know just how precious and fragile life and love really are. She was diagnosed with leukemia and began a struggle that was truly a Calvary experience for this beautiful and courageous young woman.

Throughout years of pain, hospitalization, operations, treatments, and the awesome letdowns of hoping for a cure that never came, Betsy would not give up. She continued to live life fully; to laugh in the face of hurt, even when her body probably pressured her to grimace. Betsy also continued her search for a true and noble love, because somewhere in that wonderful mind of hers, she knew that God would not let her leave this world without experiencing the joy of an unconditional love.

And he didn't. In 1992 Betsy joined the Volunteer Fire Department in Rockville Centre and in the time she had left to live responded to 287 calls. She lived this life-saving vocation until the end, going out on a fire call just days before she died. Among the firefighters with whom Betsy worked was a young man named Dave Schowerer. This delightful man was the guy Betsy had been waiting for. It was the truest kind of love. It was gentle and it was raucous. It was about laughter and about tears. It was totally honest communication, because time was too special a thing to play with. It involved long nights of sharing, talking until dawn because there was so much to say and so little time left to say it. It was about being thrilled to have found that soulmate we all hope will be out there for us. Betsy knew that in Dave she had found hers, and Dave knew it too.

One summer day, Betsy and I went out to lunch. We talked about the disease—it had come back after a failed bone marrow transplant—and something in Betsy told her that this might be it. I was less amazed by her courage, which was fierce, than by her single-hearted determination to marry the man she loved. She looked across the table and said words I will never forget "I know that I may not get better, that I may have to die. But before I go, I sure would like to leave this life being married to the man I love." Being more into denial than Betsy was, I immediately downplayed the whole thing. "You're not going to die, Betsy. Don't even talk like that." But Betsy was right. Her time was coming to an end. By mid-August death was imminent. But, thank God, Betsy and Dave got their wish. Just hours before her death, Betsy and Dave were married. Their parents, watching between tears and smiles, saw their children commit themselves to be best friends forever. She died as Betsy Toy Schowerer, just as she dreamed she would.

Sometimes the young people we debunk can amaze us. They know more about love and life, commitment and caring, devotion and faithfulness than we give them credit for. Betsy taught me and so many others that life is a great gift. It's meant to be lived fully and passionately. It is too precious to waste. At the moment Betsy died, a family member who loved her deeply cried "Betsy, don't go." But Betsy's mother Pam said something different. She put her hand gently on Betsy's sister and said, "Let her go; it's all right, let her go." And her Mom was right. Betsy could go to God with a heart that smiled. She had found the meaning of true love. And she had married him.

Question for Reflection

- Betsy "knew" that God would not let her leave this world without experiencing the joy of an unconditional love. What kind of family-life experience must Betsy have had for her to have this certainty?

Reunion

I love the summer. It's a time to slow down, to get renewed, to put things in perspective. A time to be refreshed. The summer of '90 was even more special than most. Because for the Maria Regina Class of 1970, it was time for us to reunite, a time to come together and celebrate four of the best years of our lives. High school reunions are a wonderful experience. They help us to look again at where we've been and to savor the years that made us who and what we are today.

I was touched at my reunion by many of the people I met and talked with. The life experiences they've been through were awesome.

A number of our classmates are dead. Even more faculty members have passed on. Some classmates married happily; others have been married and divorced. I asked one former classmate, "So, are you married?" His response: "Oh, yes, many times!"

Some of the class are parents, others still long to be. Some have adopted children from faraway nations. Some classmates are struggling to make ends meet; others are wealthier than they ever imagined they could be back in 1970. And, interestingly, the most successful are not the ones we thought would be so many years ago. Life is like that—full of surprises.

Some of my classmates are parents of "special children"; and one has a severely handicapped young son—it was moving to see young Sean at our class reunion picnic. Another lesson in patience and charity they never mentioned in high school.

Some of the class are regular churchgoers. Some never left, and many are starting to come back with the arrival of children. They want to pass along something of value. And faith, some have come to recognize, is a deeply treasured gift. Some believe in Jesus, but not the Catholic way. These are the born-again members of the class. One classmate felt the urgent need to tell me of her "testimony." No more Catholicism for her, she had discovered "the Lord." When I told her that I, too, was "born again," she seemed surprised. "But you're a Catholic priest," she protested. "Yes," I replied, "and we know Jesus rather intimately too." Why is it, I found myself wondering, that people who "get religion" are so sure that no one else has it but them?

As the partying went on and people loosened up, it became apparent that many were experiencing pain. Many of my most joyful classmates back then are now carrying such a heavy burden—and, amazingly, are doing it without coming undone. They carry well a variety of crosses, I suspect, because of a valued lesson we were taught at Maria Regina so long ago. The lesson was simple and true. It went something like this: No matter what we do, however bad our lives may be, no matter how deeply we betray the good we know we should be living—God is there. He is loving us. And he forgives as soon as we remember. Our God, we happily learned, is a Creator of compassion, mercy and tenderness.

More than the "new math," more than modern languages, more than American literature, more than SATs, this was the message we learned and now live. Our God is a God of love, and that love is unconditional. That knowledge, that strength, that insight continues to light up our lives. It allows the drunk and divorced, the adoptive parent and the parent whose child has died, the millionaire and the jobless, the health enthusiast and the fellow who lives dialysis to dialysis, the priest and the born-again, the never married and the many-times-married to come together. To celebrate. To hope. To remember.

And somewhere that weekend the things that really matter became clear. It happened whenever a wallet was opened to show baby pictures. It happened every time someone listened attentively to someone else's pain. It happened when the kiss of peace at Mass moved from a handshake to a hug. It happened when people who saw that young handicapped boy did more than stare, but stopped over to play and to caress.

Reunions are times to remember. And the lesson we learned so long ago still holds true: that God's love forever lives on—most especially in our love for one another.

Question for Reflection

• What, if any, have been your experiences of God's unconditional love for you?

No Sacrifice at All

In the video for his best-selling song "Sacrifice," Elton John offered a visual interpretation of his music. She wants to head in new and more exciting directions. The man is left pining. He misses his spouse and longs for her return. But he's also got another need. (He must raise their baby daughter alone.) Throughout most of the video he seems overwhelmed by his situation. But by the end, as he dances with his little girl, the words "it's no sacrifice at all" take on richer meaning. Because in giving his time, his energy and his devotion to his daughter, he's discovered that sacrifice can really give meaning to life.

Another example comes to mind. Two young women, two responses. I was visiting a Catholic high school to speak about abortion. When I finished, a student rose to speak. She said words that haunted me. "Father, I agree with you, that the unborn child is a person. But, well, I'm eighteen years old, I have my whole life ahead of me. I want to go to college now. To be saddled with a child would be such a sacrifice." To which I responded, "That's true." And when another student suggested that a pregnancy could also lead to placement for adoption, yet another young woman rose to say, "It's really asking too much to expect a girl to carry a baby for nine months and then give it away." Another sacrifice too great.

The concept of sacrifice is growing steadily more unpopular. And yet I don't know if it's even possible to love another human being unless I'm open to the reality of sacrificing. It costs to love. There's no such thing as love without surrender of my personal likes and wants for sake of the mutual love.

I remember, several years ago, trying to get my one-year-old nephew to sleep. I had no success. Every time I'd put him down in the crib he'd let out a wail. This went on for hours. At one point, when he was actually being quiet, I crept out of his room. I got the door open a crack when he let out the loudest

scream yet. After what seemed like an eternity, he finally drift-
ed off to sleep. I remember asking my mother, "did we do that
too?" Of course," she replied. "How did you do it?" I asked.
"You just love more than you care about the discomfort," my
mother replied.

Everyone, it seems, wants to be a lover. But the path to true
love is sacrifice. Think about it. Carrying a child for nine
months is a sacrifice. Getting up at 5:30 a.m. every day to commute to a job you really don't like so you can pay your family's
bills is a sacrifice. Cooking meals is a sacrifice. Shopping for
your family for twenty years or so is no great joy. Holding a
sick child's head over the toilet at 3 a.m. is no treat. Sitting up
all night waiting for a maybe sober, maybe not, teenager is no
special privilege. Changing the 4,000th diaper of a baby;
removing the bedpan of an elderly parent; scrubbing the spas-
tic child who suffers from cerebral palsy—none of these are
activities any normal person would long for. And yet, everyone of these actions says "I love you" much more powerfully
than words.

And is it all worth the price, worth the sacrifice? Jodie
DiFato thinks so. She's a seventeen-year-old woman with a
child who's almost two. His name is James, and Jodie's raising
him as a single parent. She spoke to a group of us recently
about the challenge of parenting, about the lost sleep and cur-
tailed plans, about the moments of frustration and the times
when you just want to give up. And then, said Jodie, James
gives you a smile or a hug. That's all. And suddenly the sacrifice doesn't seem so bad. In fact, it's no sacrifice at all.

Question for Reflection

- "There's no such thing as love without surrender of my
  personal likes and wants for the sake of the mutual love."
  Agree or disagree? Why?

Grandparents

Years ago when I was driving along with my seven-year-old nephew, he popped me a question well beyond our usual discussion of Nintendo. "Uncle Jim," asked Matthew, "can a person die of grief?" Now, I know the kid's bright, but that was about the last question I ever expected from this second-grader. "Where," I asked, "did you hear about dying of grief?" Seems he'd seen a video cartoon called "Fearless John" in which John's friend's father died first, and then his mother died of grief. This amazed Matthew, who asked me to explain. "Well, Matthew, when people love each other deeply, it can hurt very much when someone dies. And because their hearts are broken, people sometimes lose their will to live. So, yes, I guess people can die of grief."

Matthew pondered that answer for a while and then came to an interesting conclusion. "No offense to you or my Mom or Dad, I love you, but I wouldn't die if you guys died." Then the other shoe fell. But Uncle Jim, if Grandma or Grandpa died, I think I would die of grief."

Matthew adores his grandparents, and the feeling is mutual. Matthew is not atypical. As we live longer, more and more families are spending time together. And young children are coming to know their grandparents as never before. Instead of belonging to a two-generation family, it's more likely that we'll enjoy a three- and four-generation family. And that raises an interesting issue: Do we treasure our senior citizens, especially those who make up our families?

Take a look at any popular magazine or newspaper. Look at the ads. You'll see many "beautiful people," all of them young. Where are the advertisements for the elderly? Don't they buy clothing? Don't they read the newspapers? Why are they so often treated as if they're invisible? They aren't, you know. Senior citizens are a huge sector of our society, numbering in the millions of people. They live lives of great value. Experienced in the realities of life, wise in ways that only people who've been around can be—they are a precious national resource.

And yet, in a culture directed at deifying youth, they are often forgotten or considered passé. What a mistake that is. We're told that those who don't study history are doomed to repeat its mistakes. Well, our senior citizens are a living history who can help and enrich us greatly.

Not only that, but they're also incredibly generous folks. And in the internationally troubled economic situation, they can be and often are all that stands between children and disaster. Recent studies indicate that from a strictly financial point of view, grandparents are directly supporting their children and grandchildren now more than ever. Consider the reasons why:

Less than 10 percent of American families can afford to have one parent stay home with the children while the other parent goes out of the home to work. That means that 90 percent of American parents need someone to be there for young children returning from school. In many cases, that someone is a grandparent. There are 26 million children returning from school to homes where parents are out working.

One-fourth of American children live in single-parent homes. That means that the single parent will be juggling domestic and economic demands. Filling the void, very often, are grandparents.

Ninety percent of women who divorce take custody of their children, while losing 73 percent of their annual income. Twenty-five percent of the fathers involved will never make a single child support payment.

It would be foolish, though, to limit an appreciation of grandparents to their financial generosity. The greater value they offer is their time, their wisdom, their life experience and their love.

Again and again I've talked with grandparents who tell of a similar experience. They say they enjoy their time with grandchildren more than the time they spent with their own children. Said one grandfather, "I was too busy making a living to appreciate my own kids as I should have. My grandchildren let me see parts of life I never saw before."

Grandparents have also been around the track. They've lived full and rich lives. Their lives have taught them lessons we can only benefit by knowing. So maybe we should listen to them more. Their insights into life may well save us a good deal of needless pain and error.

In a culture like ours, which celebrates the young and beautiful, the shapely and sexy, many of us miss the truest value: the insight of wisdom. That's a gift grandparents can offer and we should more readily accept. Wisdom is the ability to see, to know the heart, to understand because we've been there. So many of our grandparents have that gift in abundance. They have a richness earned over a lifetime of exploring, searching, examining. And we'd be foolish not to listen and appreciate them and their truth.

The second Sunday of September is National Grandparents Day. Bet you didn't know that. Because while we make a big-time fuss over Mother's and Father's Day, few remember to celebrate these special and necessary friends. Forgetting their value would be a foolish mistake. Because behind their aging countenances and slightly stooped frames, grandparents possess a vitality of the heart and soul that children and grandchildren need now more than ever.

Question for Reflection

- "Our senior citizens are a living history who can help and enrich us greatly." How? What role have your grandparents played in your life?

Home Alone

Did you ever watch *The Cosby Show*? Or *Growing Pains*? Or *Families Ties*? They're shows which were made in the 1980s and '90s but aren't a whole lot different from programs produced in the 1950s. Check out your cable station's reruns. Each show begins with a family problem. And every show ends with the family problem solved. In a half hour every human difficulty is resolved. Amazing, isn't it? And just like real life, right? Well, not exactly. At least not in the families I know.

The truth is, nobody's family has it altogether. We're all in need of improvement. And recognizing that can be a liberating feeling. Some years ago, there was a bestselling book by a Dr. Thomas A. Harris called *I'm O.K.—You're O.K.* It sold like hotcakes. But when you're writing about American family life today, maybe it's better to say, "We're not O.K., and they're not O.K.—and that's O.K." Accepting our limits and imperfections is a healthy thing to do. Because between failed materialism and epidemic divorce, the multiplication of single-parent homes, the increase in emotional and physical abuse, the incidence of drug and alcohol abuse, the economic downturn with high unemployment, and the fact that 22 million children return home each day to empty homes, we're dealing with a stressed-out concept of family in the third millennium.

So what do we do about it? Should we give up? Well, of course not. Family doesn't have to be perfect to have incredible value. We've got to take the families we've been given and make them the best they can be.

And how do we do it? Let's start with some basics:

(1) *Spending quality time together.* Recent studies tell us that the average American family, if they eat together at all, is finished with dinner in ten to fifteen minutes. That's not only bad for digestion, it's a poor way to relate to people we love. Let's go for a minimum of half an hour. And that means no television or reading at the table. Eating and talking only!

(2) *Praying together.* Years ago there was an expression that went like this: "The family that prays together, stays together." Sounds corny right? But, you know, it may be one of those old-fashioned ideas that holds true. Let me put it to you this way: I deal with families all the time. I have yet to meet a family that goes to Mass together, says grace before meals together, says the rosary together or reads the Bible together who are worse off because of it. On the contrary, it seems to me that families who let God into their lives are stronger, more unified and better able to deal with the inevitable stresses of modern-day living.

(3) *Get "riches" straight.* When I do marriage preparation, I often ask the engaged couples if they intend to have children. They usually say yes, but not for a while. And when I ask them how many they'll have, they say, "Maybe one or two." And if you ask them why not three or four, they say, "We want to be able to give our children the best." But who says giving them "the best" isn't giving another brother or sister? And who convinced us that material comfort is more important than family? No car, no home, no thing can match the value of a person, a brother, a sister, a child. If we lose that sense of perspective, we lose the real value of family.

(4) *Say the words that matter.* There's no time like the present to say the things we should. We're people, and people need to say and to hear words that matter. Like "I love you" and like "I'm sorry." Five simple words, but too infrequently uttered in many families. Say them soon. They're the glue for good family living.

Questions for Reflection

- Name ways in which your family could (a) spend quality time together; (b) pray together.
- How do you sometimes fail/sometimes succeed in saying the words that matter?

From a Distance

L et me make a confession. Most of you have done something that I only recently tried for the first time. I cooked a meal. No big deal, just a little chicken, some vegetables, a few potatoes, gravy and a salad. Nothing went right. The chicken was undercooked, the vegetables limp, the mashed potatoes loaded with lumps. Only the salad made sense.

I came away from the experience with a new appreciation for the miracle of meal making. I think the toughest part was having everything ready at the same time. How do you do that? I mean, getting all the items ready (and hot) at the same time.

Sixteen years of school and all I had was pink chicken and cold potatoes. Made me think about all the years I'd sat down to eat without giving a thought to how the meal was prepared. I never was filled with wonder at the sight of a good meal; now I'm absolutely amazed at anyone who can pull it all together! I'd been looking at food and the people who prepared it from a distance.

No one in my family is a big drinker. We had no one with an alcohol problem. So alcoholics were like foreigners to me as a kid. I heard about them on television. Read stories about famous "drunks" like F. Scott Fitzgerald. And came to see them as poor fools who obviously chose to make other people's lives miserable. I never thought in terms of their burden, or their having a disease.

And then I became friends with a wonderful young man named David. He is good and kind and loving. But sometimes he drinks too much. He's a bonafide alcoholic who's lucky to be alive. He hates being drunk, hates what it does to his family and loved ones. Knows that if he keeps it up he will die. He struggles, every day, with this awful and painful illness.

He does not (as I'd thought) choose to be alcoholic. It is a disease, and it's not easily licked. I never knew that until I knew David—a real person like millions of others, who longs to be free from the prison of addiction. Until David, I was seeing alcohol and alcoholics from a distance. My vision was a blur. Now I understand the cross which is alcoholism.

Pregnancy in my family was an occasion for rejoicing. Every child, every baby a joyous blessing. I never knew what it is to grieve at the news "you're pregnant." And coming from a place where babies were desired and treasured made something like abortion unthinkable. It was a heinous idea and an unthinkable crime.

Then it was legalized. Millions of women chose to kill their children. Seeing children as a gift made the notion of abortion a mystery for me. And sometimes, I'm afraid, my heart was hard against those who decided to abort. I simply could not see what would lead a person to destroy a child. The decision seemed so senseless, so very violent. I would have found it hard, if not impossible, to love a person who could choose to end a baby's life.

And then something happened I never imagined. They certainly never taught us about it at the seminary. I sat in confession one rainy Saturday afternoon, ordained maybe three months. Most of the confessions were not that unusual. And then a woman I knew came in. She was not young, had a slew of children, and was a woman I liked very much. I expected a confession of some impatience, a little anger perhaps, nothing more. And then she said it.

Over twenty years ago she had aborted her child. An unexpected pregnancy, being unmarried, fear of parental response, shame at what people would say, not having much money, all these were reasons for the abortion. They mattered less to me than the sight of this good woman absolutely ravaged by the pain of her action. She had lived a seeming eternity with a suffering that would not go away. She loved her other children, but always remembered that there had been one before them. She wept uncontrollably.

I rose and went to her side. We embraced and she rocked with sobs of anxiety and relief, emotions interspersed in a way only God's grace could foment.

That moment changed me. Oh, it didn't make abortion any more palatable. It still fills me with an aching sorrow. But now abortion had a human face. Now I saw the aborted mother not as a "bad" or evil person. I saw her as a pain-filled and confused pilgrim stumbling on the road to healing and wholeness.

Up until that moment, I was seeing abortion and those who tragically choose it only from a distance. Up close, you see two victims instead of one. And it breaks your heart even more.

Many years ago Bette Midler produced a striking album called *Some People's Lives*. And, by far, the highlight of the many songs she offers is her hit "From a Distance." It focuses on the way perceptions change depending on where you sit. Up close or far away makes all the difference. Looking down at someone or sitting at their side. Being involved or being but a passive observer.

I love most of the song, but disagree with one key verse. Midler tells us that "God is watching us, from a distance." No offense, Bette, but I think you've got it wrong. Love, understanding, appreciation, respect, forgiveness, compassion and genuine knowledge only happen when we get close. God is the perfection of these qualifies. He is the closest. He never watches from a distance. And when we bother to see and taste and feel up close, we glimpse something of the Divine.

Intimacy is a holy project. And I'm convinced that we cannot be completely close to our wondrous Creator until we begin to see life from up close. People are so easy to hate, to judge, to dismiss and to minimize until we get within touching distance. Only then do we get a true hint of the soul.

And how close does God get? "Footprints" says it best: "One night a man had a dream. He dreamed he was walking along the beach with our Lord. Across the sky flashed scenes from his life. For each scene he noticed two sets of footprints. One belonged to him and one to the Lord. When the last scene flashed before him, he looked back and noticed that during the lowest and most difficult times of his life there was only one set of footprints. This really bothered him, and he questioned our Lord. Lord, you said that once I decided to follow you, you would walk all the way with me. But during the hardest times of my life I see only one set of footprints. Where were you when I needed you the most, Lord? The Lord replied, My precious, precious child. I love you and would never leave you. But during your times of pain and trial and suffering, where you see only one set of footprints, it was then that I carried you."

Questions for Reflection

- A "Peanuts" cartoon character once said, "I love mankind; it's people I can't stand." How does that apply here?
- Recall a time when you were troubled and thought God was absent, only to realize afterwards that God had been "carrying" you the whole time.

On Fear and Love

A priest expects to visit the sick. It comes with the job, and is one of the reasons you become a priest to begin with. Like most of my brothers, I've visited many, many people afflicted with any number of infirmities. I'm not usually frightened when I visit a person who is ill, but one time I was terrified.

My friend Roseann called and asked me to visit her friend Adam. Sure, I replied, what hospital is he in? "He's not in a hospital," she replied. "He's beyond any help." "What's the matter with him?" I asked. "He's dying of cancer, and he has AIDS," Roseann said.

The next few days were paralyzing. I've read as much as anyone about AIDS. I've even preached on it, naming it as a "great tragedy." But now I was going to meet the illness face to face. And, I'd be a liar if I didn't admit to absolute ignorance and prejudice. I looked for a dozen reasons to cancel my appointment with Adam. After all, what would I say to him, how would I relate to him and what about the risks? Whenever I visit a sick person I touch them. I hold their hands, I anoint them, and often I kiss them on the forehead. Surely, all those human touches were out of the question.

But, failing to find a good enough reason to cancel, I went to visit with Adam. All of my worst fears were realized quickly. He looked horrible, a skeleton of a man. His body was scarred with lesions, the apartment was still but smelled of illness. And, sure enough, I was no sooner in his presence, than he extended his weakened hand. Instinctively I grabbed it, flinching with ignorant fear inside. He coughed a bit, and I held my breath. I sat and secretly wondered if the chair was contaminated. I gave in to all my fears, all my anxieties, all my ignorance. You don't catch AIDS from a chair, from a hand extended in welcome, from a cough. I knew all that in my head, but fear really screwed up good judgment. In a desperate attempt to make conversation and to channel my nervous energy, I got up to view the many photographs that lined the bedroom walls.

Pointing to what I thought might be his parents, I asked, "How are they dealing with all this?" "Not well," he answered. Then I came to another photo of a strikingly handsome young man, tan, in shape and with a blazing smile. "Your brother?" I asked. "No, Father Jim, that guy is me, last year." My heart sank, my eyes filled, and I blurted out, "I'm so sorry, Adam."

Something in that moment freed me. The life-altering pain and brokenness of this young man stilled my foolish fears. I sat again and we talked for hours. I held his hands without fear, I anointed him no more carefully than I would anyone else, and when I left, I kissed him gently on the forehead, grateful for the opportunity to have been with this courageous man who had accepted and cooperated with God's incomprehensible will.

I got back to my rectory and passed a bathroom on the first floor. Instinctively I moved to wash my hands, a reactive fear coming over me. But as I looked into the mirror I saw the greatest lesson of that visit with Adam. We are, all of us, like Adam. Human, frail, needful, dependent, sometimes beautiful, sometimes difficult to face, we are all, at times, difficult to love, to embrace, to accept. But, you know, if we can, with God's help, bring ourselves to kiss the Adams of this world, then we never need be afraid of anyone or anything again. Dear Adam, thank you for the lesson about living, and about dying, about fear and about freedom. May he rest in peace.

Question for Reflection

- What can help you to overcome your fear and distaste of visiting a very sick person?

Living Together

Like most brothers, I've had a fair number of battles with my sisters. We don't agree on everything; and we sometimes see the world with widely different visions. But I love them and I know they love me, so we can forgive the places we part company.

There is one issue, though, on which we share common ground, and that's on the idea of couples living together before marriage. Throughout my years in the seminary, I always wondered and worried about the guys my sisters dated. I'm sure most brothers are a little critical about the people who date their sisters. Because even though our sisters may be a pain at times, they are people we care deeply about. And we don't want them being taken advantage of by other men. Maybe it's that we know our own selfish instincts are to use the people we date, and we project the same values on to our sisters' boyfriends. But for whatever reasons, we do cast a wary eye on the fellows they bring home.

Sometimes, after a period of dating, couples make a decision to live together before marriage. That was a fear I never saw fulfilled with my sisters. They seemed smart enough to realize the dangers in living together. Couples who do move in together sometimes couch the decision in terms of practical considerations. They blame it on economic necessity, saying it will "save them money." Others say it will "give them more quality time together." Some say it can help them find out if they're compatible.

I had this discussion recently with a girl I know. She told me that she and her boyfriend were living together to ascertain if they were "well matched." If they could handle the daily problems they faced then they'd know if marriage was for them. She also said they would discover more about their "sexual compatibility." And, she added, can you imagine how horrible it would be to marry someone and then discover that "you didn't find them sexually fulfilling!"

Such reasoning offers lots of false confidence. Anyone can "play house." And living together can be a novel notion, for a while. But there really is no foolproof way to anticipate the challenges of marriage. Marriage is an act of faith. It can't be planned or programmed. And no amount of "practice" can prepare you for the living of it. Ask anyone you know if they ever anticipated what marriage would be like; then ask them if their expectations matched the reality. Most will tell you there's a world of difference between the distant vision and the day-in and day-out experience of living as a married couple, as a family.

And statistics seem to bear this out. Recent studies indicate that while the national rate of divorce is very high, it's even higher for couples who live together before marriage. The reason for that, I think, is twofold. First, living together can give couples that false confidence of feeling that they really know what marriage is all about. In fact, they only know about sharing common space. Sharing committed love is not the same as cohabitation. Secondly, the privileged experience of sharing the marriage covenant is badly served by trying it out first. Most couples see their wedding day as a unique and precious moment of a new and different commitment. But if they've already been living like a married couple, then what's the sacredness of marital commitment really all about? It becomes, no more than a contract moment wherein something informal is formalized.

The issue of living together also raised the thorny issue of what sex before marriage means for us. Couples who live together (and engaged couples) have sex on a regular basis. They relate sexually because they believe that their love makes it okay. They don't seem to feel that sacramental commitment is required. So believing that "love is all you need," couples share one of the deepest parts of themselves with each other. But consider this: If love is all you need before marriage to allow for sexual sharing, then what do we need to justify sex with someone else after we're married? So, for example, how does a wife who finds her husband involved with another woman respond when he justifies his sexual activity by saying, "But I really love this other woman." If marriage is just a legal or formalizing moment and if "love is all you need," then why can't we have multiple sexual partners after marriage?

See, we can't have it both ways. We can't say that sexual encounter is all right simply because I love this other person. Along with the love must come a spirit of real commitment. And for those of us who call ourselves Catholic, that means the Sacrament of Marriage.

Sex is a precious and wonderful gift of God. But it's so important, and such a privilege, that it's meant to be shared in the context of committed and permanent love. Living together trivializes the power and seriousness of our commitment. And sex before marriage reduces the rights we have after marriage, to expect fidelity from our spouse. There are many terrific ways to demonstrate love before marriage, but living together is not one of them. It's bad for the soul, bad for the future of a relationship and a pretty certain way of reducing in stature a relationship worth infinitely more than "playing house."

Questions for Reflection

- "There are many terrific ways to demonstrate love before marriage, but living together is not one of them." What are some of the ways?

- What reasons can you give for or against living together before marriage?

Guys

Not long ago, I was invited to speak at a boys high school in New Jersey. There are about five hundred students and they asked me to speak about sexual responsibility. I thought I might get further in initiating a dialogue with the guys if the teachers weren't breathing down their necks. So I asked the faculty to give me forty-five minutes alone with the student body.

My first question told me a lot about my audience. I asked how many of these five hundred had ever had sex with a girl. Almost every hand went up. Now, I know that we're supposed to be living in the middle of something like a sexual revolution, but I wasn't buying the macho bluster. Not from these Catholic boys anyway. So I asked a fellow in the first row to stand. He was a sophomore named Jason. He couldn't have weighed more than eighty pounds soaking wet. And I said, looking him right in the eyes, "Jason, you mean to tell me that you've been physically involved with a woman." Looking back at me with nervous eyes, and with a voice close to cracking from the alterations of puberty, Jason replied: "Well, almost."

You see, Jason never had sex. Neither did most of the guys in that assembly hall. So why, you may wonder, would they lie? Well, for most guys it's not really lying. It's more like protecting an image. And guys care a lot about image. Not only when 499 other guys are watching, but especially when girls are around. So they say a lot of things that are supposed to make them look bigger than they are. They con. They stretch the truth, a lot. And one of their tools in deception is love. Guys know that girls love to be loved. So they pour it on. And, if their con touches the right mark, they may find themselves with both a new girlfriend and the opportunity for sexual explorations.

High school and even college-aged guys I know, when their guard is down, tell me the truth about words of love. They admit that they're really not much in love. But they are in lust. And you don't get much lust without words of love. Problem is, the young women believe the rap. They think that words of love are the same thing as love. They want to believe that words of love are the same as commitment. And of course they aren't.

So love happens. Or at least lust happens. And when it does, a part of us changes. Sometimes all we take away from lust mistaken for love is a feeling of being stupid. Sometimes we do some serious heart damage. And sometimes a baby happens. Well, not just sometimes—but 1.1 million times a year in America. Half of those babies won't get out of this romance alive. They'll be aborted. The other half will be born and end up being raised by a young mom or adopted by couples who want to parent a child. And where will "daddy" be during all this? Not real close, in most cases.

In six out of ten cases a boyfriend will help his pregnant girl-friend to get an abortion. And that's to his benefit because aborting a baby will only cost him about $400. But if his girl-friend delivers and keeps the baby, Dad will be obligated to pay child support for at least eighteen years.

In eight out of ten cases, once a young woman chooses to have her baby instead of aborting, her boyfriend splits. Only two in ten young men stay supportive through pregnancy, delivery and the first six months of the child's life. And from where I sit, these facts say a big "shame on you" to the guys. Guys talk a good game, but boy are we awful on the delivery.

It takes two people to make a baby. Two. And if a guy's not ready to welcome, support, nurture, finance and love the third person created by the two, then he should hang back until he grows up.

P.S.: I don't want to blow off the two guys in ten who accept and live real responsibility. Such men are not boys, but mature adults worthy of praise and support. I just wish that the Jasons of the world would get with the program and stop talking sex until they include a genuine understanding for women, and a committed love for the children who oftentimes pop into existence when we decide to follow our hormones instead of our consciences.

Questions for Reflection

- To guys: How would you react to the news that your girlfriend was pregnant because of you?
- To girls: What can be the results when we "follow our hormones instead of our consciences"?

"Boom, Boom, Boom"

Driving out east one Sunday morning I listened to the top 40 songs of the week. When we got to the superhits, the top five, I heard the words of a song which certainly deserved an award for directness. The refrain went like this:

"Boom, boom, boom, let's us go back to my room, where we can do it all night, and you can make me feel right."

I continued to listen, wondering if the guy singing the song would develop the relationship beyond "boom, boom." He doesn't. And, sadly, neither do most guys.

In my work at the Family Ministry Office I got calls each week from teenage girls who found themselves in crisis pregnancy situations. They were looking for support and understanding. I would try to see them right away because I knew that the pressure on them to "get rid of it" is enormous. And I always invited them to bring along their boyfriend, the father of the child. In almost eight out of ten cases the young woman showed up alone or with a girlfriend; sometimes with her mother or a sister. When I asked her where her boyfriend was, the response was often, "He doesn't want to be involved," or "He wants me to get rid of it," or "He said he'd give me money for an abortion," or "He said, how do I know it's his?"

What we're dealing with here is what I call the "wimp factor." Guys, filled with macho braggadocio, talk a good game to assure their girlfriends of their undying love before and during a sexual touchdown. But bring a child into the picture, and you're more than likely going to see the tail end of their horses.

Teenage sexual activity almost necessarily lacks a sense of responsibility and of a permanent commitment to the other person. For the sexually active teen male, the tendency to cut and run when crisis challenges us to stick around and face the problem is nothing less than an admission of one's emotional inadequacy. Somewhere between "boom, boom" and a baby there's got to be a sense of owning what I do, accepting the consequences of my choices.

So before I decide (or let my body decide for me) to share myself completely with another human being, I've got to be real sure that I can live with the results of that sexual encounter. One of the best ways to check out the rightness or wrongness of what we do with our bodies is to ask ourselves some questions: Can I seriously see myself spending a lifetime with this particular person with whom I'm about to become involved? Could I ever really imagine being married to this presently attractive person? Can I begin to see myself as a Dad or Mom? Do we have the financial means to support a child? Can I handle the mental and social stress of being a parent at my age? Would I be able to handle telling my parents that I'm pregnant or that I've helped someone to become pregnant? Putting it directly: Can I live with the consequences of sex beyond the "feel good" part of it? If my answer to these questions is no, then I'm probably also discovering the answer to the question of my readiness for sex right now. And so to anyone offering the experience of "boom, boom," the smart teenager will say, "Thanks, but no thanks."

Question for Reflection

- Whether you are 16 or 66 the question is valid: Can you live with the consequences of sex (outside of marriage) beyond the "feel good" part of it?

Part III

More of Both

Young and Stupid

The college I attended had a definite set of rules. And some of them were strictly enforced. One of the more serious violations involved having or using alcohol on campus. That was forbidden. And breaking the rules, the handbook told us, meant expulsion.

When you're young, rules, even if strictly written, aren't taken seriously. They're made to be broken or, at least, avoided—because when you're young, you can really come to believe that you're invincible. Nothing can really get you. Nothing can do you in. You believe in your personal ability to bounce, to prosper in the face of adversity.

Well, in my senior year I believed in my total ability to dance around the rules. I was student body president and thought I was very important. Rules certainly didn't apply to me or my friends. So one night, after a bit of outside celebrating, a bunch of us went back to my room to continue the party. Drinks were served and a good time was had by all. But at one lull, I noticed that we were running low on ice cubes. Thought I'd go fetch some more and then continue partying. After all, what could happen in the five minutes I'd be away?

Well, plenty happened. When I returned my door was wide open. Not a promising sign for our private party. And all my friends had fled. Actually, they'd been sent to their rooms. And there, in the middle of the room, picking up bottles and beer cans was the monsignor who ran the college. He didn't look happy, and I felt my stomach go right to my feet. I tried to explain, but what could I say? This was a bold-face violation of the rules. This was big-time trouble. This was "hasta la vista, baby." Monsignor Tom said very little. We wouldn't talk now, he said, but in the morning at his office.

I didn't sleep much that night. I knew that I was out and wondered if my friends were to be given the gate, too. You start to think about your parents and how disappointed and embarrassed they're going to be. You beat yourself up a lot and wonder if the trouble you're in was worth the few hours of "partying." And dumb as you feel, you also know that there's nothing you can do. You blew it. You failed. You were incredibly stupid. And in my particular case, I knew it might also mean that I'd never get to be a priest. The priesthood wasn't everything back then but was important enough to miss when you realize that it's lost out of sheer foolishness. I mean, losing it all for an important cause is one thing, but for beer!

I got up early the next morning and prepared for the "goodbye" meeting with Monsignor Tom. When I arrived at his office, I was left outside to wait for what seemed like eternity. Then I was ushered into his somber presence, waiting for the ax to fall. He told me that what I had done was very dumb. He told me he was woefully disappointed in me. He said I had set a miserable example by my actions. He told me I had violated the rules of the college. All of this I expected. I had no defense. He was right. I was a jerk. But then he ended with a much unexpected closing! "Stop being irresponsible. Think about the consequences of your actions. Be a positive role model for others. And grow up. From this moment on, Mr. Lisante, this incident is closed and over. Don't let it happen again."

If I was smart I would have thanked him very much and made for the door. But I guess I was in shock. After all, I had mentally packed my bags. So I asked him the question: "Why are you doing this? Why are you giving me another chance?" Monsignor Tom's answer said as much about him as it did about me: "Because, Jim. I haven't forgotten that I was once young and stupid, too."

I learned a lot about compassion that day. I learned a lot about walking in the shoes of people we'd sooner judge and condemn. I learned that none of us is beyond a second, or a third or even a fourth chance. And I learned that we all, in the end, have clay feet. So who are we to be harsh with each other?

Only years later, as I was preparing a homily on the gospel of the woman caught in the sin of adultery, did I come to see the meaning of my partying experience in college. Jesus tells the stone-crazed crowd to back off unless they are sinless. Of course, no one is. He doesn't condemn the guilty woman but challenges her to change, to be better. That's what Monsignor Tom Gradilone did for me. And I'm a better man for his kindness.

It's so easy to judge, to condemn, to be above others. But in the end, we're all struggling with the same fragile humanity. And if we can just avoid giving up on one another, what a wondrous world we could become.

Questions for Reflection

- Supposing you had been given this kind of second chance. What would you have learned from the experience?

- If you had been in Monsignor Tom's position, would you have given a second chance? Why or why not?

Getting Off the Ride

I hate being trapped. And I remember a ride at the Rye Beach amusement park that always made me feel trapped. It was called "the Steeplechase," and it moved with what seemed to me as a kid to be incredible speed. Once you got on it, there was no getting off. If you tried to break away in the middle of the ride, you'd be a goner. It was like being at the top of the first huge hill on the roller coaster, and wondering why you ever got on the stupid ride, and knowing that there is no exit now. The only way out is down.

I ran into my high school classmate, Dave, recently. He was someone we "partied" with. We all move through the partying experiences of life. Dave did not. Alcohol and drugs were for him a ride he couldn't get off.

We all presume, I think, that experimenting is something we all go through. We believe that we will have our good times and then move on. As a priest, though, I've seen another side of partying. I stay in touch with a lot of my high school classmates. I celebrate their weddings, baptize their children and bury their loved ones. And staying in touch has allowed me to see that many friends, like Dave, never moved past the alcohol, the drugs, the partying. Their development as people is arrested during high school, they get trapped and hooked on ways of living that permanently alter their future.

In most cases they did not get "hooked" all by themselves. They were introduced to their poison by people they called "friends." But the truth is that anyone who promotes the need for me to alter my state of consciousness (read: getting high) in order to find happiness is a liar. Such people are really a bed of quicksand posing as friends.

Because, you see, we really don't know who of our friends can, and who can't, handle drugs and alcohol, so that when I push the partying scene it's really not unlike promoting a game of Russian roulette. Somebody will be hurt, and hurt badly. I am sure that my high school friends thought that Dave, like the rest of us, could party and then move on with his life. But he didn't. He couldn't. And we, who encouraged him to party, were really placing Dave over a trap door that would inevitably collapse. And collapse it did.

His drinking and drugging made college impossible; he dropped out after a semester. He has never been able to keep a job. He never really developed skills for a career. His interpersonal relationships all self-destructed. I know that Dave often gives way to despair. He's attempted suicide.

And when I see Dave I always want to cry. We were there at the beginning. We could have been a way out if we'd only recognized the signs. But we didn't or couldn't. We presumed that he was just like us, and he isn't. And, in moments of intense honesty, we have to face our responsibility. We all helped to joyride our friend down a road of self-destruction. We just never considered the consequences of our partying. True friends do.

True friends are sensitive to the effects their actions have on those they care for. We should have noticed that Dave needed to party too much. We should have seen that for him, partying wasn't a lark, it was a necessity. And when he was in need of money for drugs or alcohol, we should have had the courage to say no. Not to supply him.

For Dave and for perhaps as many as 20 to 30 percent of our friends, drugs and alcohol are the "Steeplechase," the ride they just can't get off. Real friends do all they can to keep those we love from ever getting on that ride toward no exit.

Question for Reflection

- How can you help the Daves in your life who can't tolerate partying?

Pornography: We All Lose

Before I was ordained, I worked for several years as a director of religious education in an urban parish. Part of the job, owing to my status as the only man on the school staff, was to spend time with the more "difficult" young people. I remember one student in particular, a boy named Charlie. He was in the eighth grade of the parish school and had been caught in class with some of the raunchiest pornography you can imagine. He was "sharing" it with his classmates and was mildly stunned when his teacher seized the goods! Charlie and I went for a walk. I purposely tried to relate in a relaxed way with him. I talked as if I found the porno as interesting as he did. And after befriending him, I mentioned that I knew people who dealt in these kinds of magazines and videos. Charlie was thrilled. To think that what he thought was going to be a strident lecture was turning into an opportunity to secure newer goods! And then, the conversation took a more surprising turn for our friend Charlie:

Charlie: "So you know where to get more of this stuff?"

Lisante: "Sure. I even know the people who publish it."

Charlie: "That's great!"

Lisante: "Yeah. In fact they're always looking for new people to put in their magazines. How would you feel about them putting a picture of your sister in, Charlie? Or your mother?"

Charlie: "That's really gross."

Yes, Charlie, it is. Only I wanted you to know that every person used by the pornography industry is a member of someone's family. In the midst of "enjoying" pornography, do we ever stop to think about that? Do we ever stop to consider how we would feel if we saw someone we love being used to tantalize? It's important to recognize that when we purchase or rent pornography, whether in magazines or videos or cable, we are paying people to dehumanize someone's daughter, someone's son, someone's sister, or someone's brother. We're reducing a human person to the level of an item we can buy. The person who appears in a pornographic enterprise becomes a "thingified" object, whose dignity is severely compromised.

Sometimes the feminist and pro-life movements seem locked in opposite directions. Our reaction to pornography, however, is a source of unity. We all seem to acknowledge that this industry, which takes in some $8 billion a year in America alone, is a violation of the intent of the First Amendment of our Constitution. Clearly, our founding fathers never intended the word "freedom" to protect those who peddle flesh and degrade the personhood of people very much like us. Of particular concern is the "kiddie-porn" industry which continues to flourish in our nation. This vile destruction of the dignity of our young reduces the child/victim to a depravity unparalleled in modern times. And yet, amazingly, the American Civil Liberties Union sees even this abomination as a "protected and fundamental right."

To be truly pro-life involves a commitment to the whole person, from conception through natural death. Our fidelity to respect for life is made particularly manifest in our willingness to protect and defend the quality and dignity of all human life. Whenever a person is compromised through the pornography industry, we are all diminished. We are not just a piece of meat. We are a reflection of our Creator. Pornography mocks God in that it violates the beauty of his handiwork.

Question for Reflection

• What is your best response to someone who suggests that pornography isn't a bad thing?

Ten Commands, Not Suggestions

A while back, I had lunch with a teenage friend, Mark, who was just out of high school. As we reviewed the highlights of his recent life, much of the discussion focused on sex. He's been pretty active. When I asked him if his conscience was bothered by having sex with people he didn't really love, he looked perplexed. His answer said a lot about where we're at now: "How can you feel bad about something everybody does?"

Mark doesn't know about objective wrong. Like many young people, his sense of morality is formed principally by peers and by what he sees reflected in the popular culture (TV, movies, internet, music). No one has told him that there are standards of behavior that are tried and true. That there are clear and definite guidelines established by God. That these laws have helped people to live moral lives for thousands of years.

These rules for living are known as the Ten Commandments. Mark could only name four, and they were recalled from childhood memory. No one had mentioned them to him in many years. That's too bad, because they make sense, and they're as relevant today as they were in the time of Moses. Maybe it would be good to recap them, using a contemporary prism.

(1) "I am the Lord your God. You shall have no gods except me." Here we're told that there is only one source of our being. It's God. We can't and shouldn't replace him with material things. He is our ultimate higher power. And we shouldn't second-guess him. He is the source of all we are and all we hope to be. Also part of this commandment is, "You shall not worship false gods." Many people treat money or sex or pop stars as if they were the ultimate high. Many people truly worship these things. Many people start to "adore" their favorite movie star, singer or television personality. Some people act as if the

sun rises on their favorite athlete. Some folks behave as if money or sex or drugs were the meaning of life. God's telling us that these are all bogus. Only God should be worshiped. Only God should be viewed as totally worthy of awe.

(2) "You shall not take the name of God in vain." This means that the name of God is sacred. It's wrong to treat the name of someone we love with disrespect. So, for example, "dammit" should never be used as if it were God's last name. And "Jesus Christ" should be an expression of praise, not a way of expressing anger.

(3) "Remember the Sabbath day and keep it holy." Every day is a new chance to thank God for the gift of life. But at least one day a week should be put aside for prayer and reflection. For us, that's Sunday. We're given 168 hours of life every week. And the Lord asks that we give at least an hour back a week to celebrate his presence in our lives. We find the time to eat, to sleep, to hang out, to study, to work and to be with people we love. So, finding an hour for God shouldn't be so hard to do.

(4) "Honor your father and your mother." They oftentimes seem like a habitual pain, but parents are (in most cases) the best friends we'll ever have. They will probably be around long after our school friends have moved on. We may not always agree with them, but parents deserve our love and respect.

(5) "You shall not kill." A human life is an unrepeatable miracle. It's wrong to destroy a person made in God's image and likeness. God is the author of life, and so only God has the right to bring life to completion. When we kill, we decide to "play God." That's not our role. Killing life, born or unborn, is just plain wrong.

(6) "You shall not commit adultery" means that if you're married, you should only be having sex with your wife or husband. And it means that if you're not married, you shouldn't be having sex with anyone.

(7) "You shall not steal." We're not supposed to take what we don't own. We're not supposed to "lift" what doesn't belong to us. And whether you call it stealing or "ripping off" doesn't change the action. If it doesn't belong to me, I should keep my hands off it.

(8) "You shall not bear false witness." This means we're wrong to lie. We were given the gift of speech to tell the truth. Lying, even the ones we call "white lies," is unacceptable. Most people lie to get out of a jam, to cover themselves. The right thing to do is tell the truth.

(9 and 10) Both have to do with "coveting." "You shall not covet your neighbor's wife." "You shall not covet your neighbor's goods." To covet means I want what you have. It can manifest itself through envy, jealousy, slander, or outright theft. It's basically saying I can't be happy unless I try to take what someone else has.

You may look at these commands as outdated. You may believe that our permissive morality is more to your liking. But these rules have guided civilization for thousands of years. They didn't last for nothing; they last because they work. If we live by these standards, we can lead happier, more productive and more honorable lives. Try them and see.

Question for Reflection

- Do you agree that the Ten Commandments are "as relevant today as they were in the time of Moses"? Why or why not?

Confession

I did something recently that most Catholics dread. I went to confession. And if statistics are correct, my nervousness is shared by most Catholics. In fact, studies indicate that well over half the people who call themselves Roman Catholic never go to confession. For most, their last experience was when they were confirmed. Going to confession for me and for most folks, is not an easy thing to do. It involves examination of who we are and what we do. It involves the humbling experience of telling another human being that we're sinners. It means asking for forgiveness, a true test of our pride. And yet, stomach knots and all, it's a good and necessary part of the Christian life.

The respected Protestant psychoanalyst Erik Erikson claimed that Catholics have an unfair advantage over Protestants because of confession. He viewed the Sacrament of Penance as therapeutic because it gives us the chance to articulate necessary guilt. That, he argued, is a healthy thing for all human beings.

When people avoid confession they often use this line of rationalization: "Why should I have to tell my sins to a priest? I can talk directly to God." The notion of confession to a priest was not an idea created by some parish priest with nothing to do. It was, in fact, initiated by Christ himself. In sending forth his apostles, our first priests, he said it clearly: "If you forgive people's sins, they are forgiven; if you hold them bound, they are held bound" (Jn 20:23). I suspect our Lord knew of the healing power of person-to-person contact. The priest is not just there to judge our sinfulness, but sits before us, as Father Henri Nouwen wrote, as a "wounded healer." He journeys with us through our guilt and remorse not as a person who is perfect, because he isn't. He is, instead, a sinner who can empathize with the struggles we each face.

In fact, when we hear horror stories about priests who used to harshly condemn or castigate penitents, we're hearing of the sacrament as it was never intended to be experienced. The model for any priest blessed with the grace to forgive sins should be (a) the Prodigal Son parable and (b) the story of the woman caught in adultery.

In the first instance the father of the sinful son demonstrates unconditional love and forgiveness for the son who has messed up. In that Gospel, we never hear the father argue that his son can come back with terms or conditions. There are no ifs, ands or buts expressed. He's just happy to have his son on the road to wholeness again.

In the second story, we hear Jesus avoid condemnation, but he also calls the woman to "go in peace and sin no more." He's gentle, forgiving, accepting, but also firmly determined that we can do better. He doesn't whitewash, he challenges. But he challenges with compassion. That is the role of the priest in the Sacrament of Penance.

Confession is also a sacred place. It's a place wherein we can tell all with the absolute confidence that our sins will be repeated to no one. I don't want to make priests out to be saints, because we're surely not that. But in all my years as a priest, I have never heard and (I believe) never will hear a priest betray the confidence of the sacrament. How reassuring it is to know that there's one place in the world where our weakness will be unavailable for exploitation.

If you're considering a return to the Sacrament of Penance, please keep a few practical things in mind:

(1) Tell the priest that it's been a while between visits. (2) Don't worry about remembering the words to the Act of Contrition; this isn't a test of your memory. (3) Don't hold back; there really are no sins that will shock the priest. (4) Spend some preparation time examining your conscience. Remember that sins still occupy the same categories they always have: sins of thought, word, deed or omission. (5) Know that for the

sacrament to be what it's supposed to be, it must include confession (I say my sins), contrition (I express sorrow for my
sins), penance (the priest will ask me to do some positive
action to atone for my sins) and absolution (the priest will free
me from the burdens of past sin).

In the movie *Godfather III* there are many powerful images
of the Church. But for me the most moving scene finds major
sinner Michael Corleone confessing to a cardinal. It shows us
that no one, and no thing we do, is beyond God's welcoming
embrace. It demonstrates the richness of this much misunder-
stood sacrament: that as soon as we remember our sins, God
forgets them.

Questions for Reflection

- Some say, "Why should I have to tell my sins to a priest? I
can talk directly to God." What is your reaction?

- Name an instance in your life in which you have felt Jesus
to be "gentle, forgiving, accepting, but also firmly determined that (you) can do better."

A Courageous Woman

I remember vividly my first sight of Patricia Neal. My parents, back in 1968, took us to see a movie called *The Subject Was Roses*. I thought she was fantastic. My admiration for her deepened greatly when I learned that her performance in that film followed rehabilitation from a series of serious strokes. With determination and extraordinary courage she had battled the ravages of a body and mind that were badly impaired. She had "fought the good fight" and been unwilling to let her illness destroy her. She still had a lot of living to do! During her rehabilitation she was also carrying an unborn child. The experience of childbirth is a trauma for even those in the fittest of shapes. But for a woman coming out of three major strokes, the burden of giving birth was immense. People could (and probably did) argue that the pregnancy should be terminated. But that route was never a serious possibility for Patricia Neal. She'd been down that road before. She knew it was a dead end!

The strokes were not Pat's first experience in monumental family crisis. She had a beautiful daughter named Olivia who died of complications from measles. That death was overwhelming for Pat. She also suffered from the senseless tragedy of seeing her only son injured in a car accident in New York City. The child's nurse inadvertently pushed his baby carriage into the street, and a passing car sent the child flying. Theo was brain damaged by the impact, giving Pat yet another reason to empathize with those living with disabilities.

Several years ago I asked this incredible woman to speak at a benefit for persons with disabilities. She came gladly and spoke to a packed house about the experiences of her life. And, somehow, the drama of her films seemed but a shadow of the real experiences of her life. As she left the stage I remember that the auditorium exploded. People stood and clapped and cried. They were in awe of the seeming indomitability of the human spirit.

There was, however, one tragedy about which Patricia Neal did not speak. It came up in conversation, but never in public. Back in the early 1950s Pat had an affair with a man she really loved. He was the actor Gary Cooper. She became pregnant, and for a multitude of reasons they chose to abort their child. Now, there are some notables who, when they've aborted, rationalize the experience, "It was really best for everyone," or, "I've never regretted my decision," or, "It was difficult but necessary." Pat never did that. She knew it was wrong to end life. And the clarity of what she chose to do has never been watered down or minimized. I had hoped, as I grew to know and treasure Pat as a friend, that one day she might share her experience with others. I sensed that it would be liberating for her and a true education for those who trivialize the awesome horror of abortion.

Thank God, she has.

In 1988 Simon & Schuster released her autobiography *As I Am*. Miss Neal wrote of her abortion with candor and regret. She names it as the worst mistake of her life, one she has lived to regret for many years. "For over 30 years, alone, in the night, I cried. If I had only one thing to do over in my life, I would have that baby," she writes. Patricia Neal says that she wishes she'd had the courage to have that baby. And while she recognizes that having a baby out of wedlock in the early 1950s would have been scandalous, she also voices her admiration for Ingrid Bergman who faced worldwide condemnation for conceiving her child through an extramarital relationship but who chose to give life instead of taking it, regardless of the cost. Writes Neal, "I admired Ingrid Bergman for having her son. She had guts. I did not. And I regret it with all my heart."

Patricia Neal went on to marry and have five other children. They are each precious to her. But there was a sixth child she misses dearly, whom she never had the chance to know. Her sharing is yet another powerful witness to the continuous courage of this wonderful woman. Her forthrightness may have cost her some friends in the "liberal" community who would be upset that she sees abortion for the tragedy that it is. But such displeasure won't upset this valiant soul.

A final story. One night, after a delightful dinner in New York City, I was driving Miss Neal back to the country home in which she was staying. She was speaking about some of the major crises of her life. As we sped along the parkway, another car came up fast behind us. The driver was obviously drunk or drugged, careening from side to side at a dangerous speed. Sure enough, as he passed, his car smashed us on Patricia's side. The intoxicated driver rode on while we pulled to the side of the road. People stopped to see that we were all right, and aside from frayed nerves, we were. After a while we got back in our car to continue the journey home. Incredibly, Miss Neal picked up the storytelling at the precise sentence she'd been on at the impact! (Nothing throws this lady.)

A warm, caring, compassionate and intelligent giant of a woman, Patricia Neal gives us all yet another lesson in the catechism of courage. Thank you, Patricia, for allowing us to share in the sorrow of your abortion. With your help, others may well choose life.

Questions for Reflection

- What qualities in a friend would enable you to share a deep hurt with them?
- How important is it to share your sorrow with another?

Defining Success

Bradley James had it all. Good-looking and talented, every-thing he touched seemed to be golden. Blessed with a keen intellect, Bradley was also as good as he was bright. With native athletic abilities, he was also a top-flight dancer. This gift led him to be accepted by the Joffrey Ballet Company. There he consorted with other equally privileged young men and women. With plentiful charm and rich in personality, he was never without a date. He could be seen squiring the best-looking girl at any party.

He was a "star" at every get-together, and folks never tired of his presence. With charisma and wit, Bradley was what most everyone wants to be. He had all that the world calls important: looks, intelligence, personality, sex appeal, success in his career and friends galore.

Bradley was also deeply creative. He could write, sing and play magnificently. His talents at the piano were astounding. He also wrote prose, and here, too, he excelled. Most of us, however, read only one side of Bradley James. In his unseen journals, Bradley revealed a quest, a thirst, a longing. Bradley had it all, but he still felt an emptiness.

I met Bradley at a pro-life conference. He came because he has a strong sense of outrage about things unjust. And killing unborn children seemed to him to be a violence against the innocent which no one should countenance. This was not his only justice cause—he also had great empathy for those who were imprisoned. This sensitivity led him to volunteer in youth prison ministry. Twice a week he would visit teenagers in prison and attempt to bring them some joy, some light.

Then reality called. There was money to be made, more success to achieve and opportunities to answer. Bradley James opened a restaurant in Palm Desert, California, a great place, always crowded, another wonderful life success. And still the nagging gut feeling that something was missing. On one visit to Bradley, we heard that Mother Teresa was in town. Bradley was filled with a boundless enthusiasm to see and to hear this noble soul. We went to a ghetto parish in Los Angeles where Mother Teresa would be welcoming more young women into her ever-expanding community. Mother's words to us were not too complex. She did not offer any great theological treatise. She was simple and direct. And the gist of her message was this: "You will only find happiness if you live your life for others." I turned in the pew to look at my friend Bradley. Tears rolled down his face. Not in sadness, but in a happiness I had never seen in him before. Because in that moment, Bradley found the missing piece, he discovered the truth about success. And it liberated him.

Bradley James became affiliated with the Missionaries of Charity—Mother Teresa's community—working with them in San Quentin Prison, the South Bronx, and in their orphanages and AIDS houses. He produced an internationally acclaimed CD, "Gift of Love: Music to the Words and Prayers of Mother Teresa" containing the voices of Mother Teresa and her Sisters all over the world. Bradley James is living a life with the knowledge of real success.

Many people in the Church worry about the future of vocations to the priesthood and religious life. And, in fact, shortages will hurt for a while. But I don't suspect we have to fear too much. It is, after all, God's Church. Throughout time he has touched the hearts of people like Bradley James. He has shown the Bradleys a way of great promise and great consolation. He has demonstrated that the more we pour ourselves out for others, the fuller and richer our lives become.

There are, I suspect, other people like Bradley James reading this essay. Good folks with many gifts who still feel an emptiness with the meaning of "success" as the world defines the term. Maybe, just maybe, real happiness will involve a life lived in service to the Church and God's people. It's surely worth a look.

Question for Reflection

- "You will only find happiness if you live your life for others." How could you envisage living this out in your own life?

Real Success

What is the meaning of success in life? Everyone has a different answer, but there are several common currents among contemporary teenagers and young adults. In one recent survey, young Americans identified their goals in this order:

(1) to achieve financial success and comfort;

(2) to find an attractive partner for love;

(3) to hold a position of importance or stature;

(4) to be well known;

(5) to look good.

By these standards, Dolores Hart had it all. Were she a young adult today, we'd sense that she had achieved the "American Dream."

Dolores Hart was a knockout-looking teenager who dabbled in acting throughout high school and college. A friend thought her gifts might be appreciated by the larger American community, and so her photograph and resume were mailed to talent scouts from Hollywood. One of these agents decided to drop by one of the amateur productions in which Dolores was acting. He liked what he saw and offered her a contract for a major movie company.

Dolores Hart became an American success pretty quickly. Her first few films included two in which her costar was Elvis Presley. She worked steadily and had it all. She was beautiful, wealthy, desired by a host of men, given even more promising contracts for a secure and brilliant future. Her name was known in most American homes.

But deep inside, Dolores Hart knew a troubling secret. She understood that you can "have it all" and still be empty, still be incomplete. She sensed that there had to be something more important than wealth, clothing, looks, stature or sex appeal.

Dolores began a spiritual journey that extended in an extraordinary fashion.

I visited with Dolores Hart during Holy Week. She now lives in a place called the Abbey of Regina Laudis. Her new title is Mother Dolores Hart, and she's a cloistered Benedictine Sister. In the early 1960s Dolores Hart left Hollywood. She gave away the many earthly possessions that had done so little for her and traded them in for the peace, the solace and the joy that she now lives as a devoted community member at the Abbey. Talking with Mother Dolores helped me to recognize, once again, the fleeting quality of our human "treasures" and the permanent value of a life lived in service to others.

Mother Dolores looks back at her Broadway and Hollywood years as an education, for there she learned that wealth and success are an illusion. She found that personal peace and happiness depend not on what we collect, but on what we spend on others. Her life for the past thirty years is a life lived for others. She gives that life in many ways. The center of Abbey life is prayer. And Mother Dolores (and her expanding Benedictine community) offer the gift of prayer many times each day. Their Mass and praying of the Liturgy of the Hours is an experience in the delight of praising God. It was an eye-opener for me to see a group of women who smile as they chant the Psalms. And their prayer is offered for others, for a world which surely needs prayerful assistance.

I mentioned earlier that the actress Dolores Hart was exceptionally attractive. But I should also tell you that the woman who is Mother Dolores Hart is even more striking. Her radiant eyes reflect a conviction in Christ and in his service that challenges and inspires. Her smile is full and warm. She doesn't take herself too seriously, but takes the life she's chosen very seriously indeed. You can sense that this life, lived for God and for his people, literally saved her life, because this life brought Dolores a richness she had never known in the midst of all the world's glory. Mother Dolores Hart, now a woman in her sixties, is a wealthy, successful and fulfilled person. Not, surely, in the measure of success most of us use—but by the measure of a God who grants riches that will never fade.

Question for Reflection

- "Those who find their life will lose it, and those who lose their life for my sake will find it," Jesus said (Matthew 10:39). How has this applied to Dolores Hart? How can it apply in your own life?

Life Gives Hope

Father Ken Marks is one of my dearest and oldest friends. I have learned so much from him, especially about the quality of hope.

They say that when we are ordained, the first few assignments can have a lifelong impact on what kind of priests and Christians we are likely to be for the rest of our lives. Ken Marks' first assignment was in the South Bronx. It was a desolated, burned-out, depressing neighborhood.

When I heard that Kenny was assigned there I was concerned for him. He, to the contrary, was delighted. He saw the assignment as an opportunity to bring hope and love and help to people who were physically impoverished but spiritually powerful.

Kenny followed that assignment with a stint up in Harlem. The people in his parish had so little. They seemed to struggle just to survive. Again, in the midst of great human pain, Ken was illuminated by the opportunity to bring some joy, some strength and some dignity to the hurting and the needful.

Through our friendship Ken Marks often invited me and the people from my suburban parish to become involved in helping the good people of the South Bronx and the beautiful people of Harlem. And in a testament to our belief in the richness of giving over receiving, we always came home from Kenny's parish feeling grateful for the opportunity, in some small way, to make a positive difference.

One of the things which always struck me about Kenny and many of the women and men who worked with him was their sparkling delight in the prospect of what these parishioners might yet hope to become. I never heard Kenny or the other generous people in ministry look with doubt as to God's purpose in creating the poor. They never allowed themselves to believe that it would be better for the poor if they had never been born.

Being Christian ministers meant that they were filled with hope and the joy of possibility. They recognized that the road out of vicious poverty would never be easy. They realized that often the people they worked with would climb the hill only to stumble again and again. But Kenny and his co-workers were empowered by a singular belief: if you are alive you can change, you can grow, you can be better. There is hope where there is life, and my friend Ken saw the endless and spectacular possibilities that sprang from that simple reality: life contains possibility. Only death can quell that possibility.

I knew many of the young people, the old people, the sick people, the broken people, the uneducated people, the desperately poor people of Ken's parishes. With few exceptions they wished for more from life. They would certainly not have selected to be poor, given their druthers.

But I never knew one, not one, who would have wished not to exist. Given a choice, hurting as they could be, they always seemed to choose life.

It seems that when you work for and with the poor there are two roads you can follow.

One is the road of people like Father Ken Marks. You deal in life, and you know that where there's life, there's possibility, there's the chance to make things better.

The other road is one most often taken by the hopeless. They look at poverty and illness and joblessness and brokenness and they believe that the poor would be better off if they never happened. They are purveyors of doom. They have been swamped by the human hurt around them and have wished it all away.

They are the people who promote abortion and sterilization in neighborhoods like Harlem and the South Bronx. They see the solution to poverty as the elimination and termination of the people they can "save" from being poor.

It always struck me as odd that Kenny Marks, who is the ultimate social justice Democrat, is so resoundingly against abortion. And when I would ask him why he was so vehement against abortion, he would tell me, "Jimmy, people who really love the poor don't show their concern by destroying the people they claim to care about.

"If you hate the viciousness of poverty," he would say, "then help to make it better. Abortion is forever. Abortion kills. Abortion is a senseless and hopeless path to choose."

Mother Teresa put it well when she said, "The poorest of the poor are not in my country (India); they are in places like America. Because in the midst of your wealth you do not see that the greatest poverty is to hate life. And abortion kills life. The poorest nations in the world are those who have abortion. That is the greatest poverty of all."

Questions for Reflection

- Have you had the opportunity to minister to the poor?
- Do you agree with Mother Teresa's statement concerning abortion and poverty?

Frank Capra, Catholic Christian

B ack in 1975, I had invited film director Frank Capra to New York for a fundraiser to assist disabled children. No one really believed that this three-time winner of the Academy Award for best director would make the trip from his California home. But come he did. His visit was an enormous hit, and Capra made a point of not just donating his time, but donating his money for the needy children. He was that kind of man.

Throughout the years since, he and his beloved wife Lucille were some of the most compassionate and truly Christian people I've ever known. I asked Frank to come East again in 1985 for another benefit. And again, the spry eighty-eight-year old said, "You bet." Alas, that visit was not to be.

Capra experienced the first of a number of small but potent strokes that left him bodily sound but mentally in a fog. In the years since the first stroke, I saw Frank with regularity. When I'd dress as a civilian, he looked a bit confused. But when I wore my Roman collar, he'd light up. I'm not sure he knew who this particular priest was, but he knew the signs of priesthood were friendly territory. Even in his weakened state, this man who could not utter complete sentences was able to pray the Our Father, the Hail Mary and the Glory Be.

Many commentators focused on the Americanism of Capra, on the corniness of his movie plots, on the unreasonableness of his heroes' triumph over evil. But few, if any, got to the heart of his art. He was a Christian, a Catholic Christian down to his toes. He revered the Eucharist, prayed intensely, treasured the Bible and believed. So important was his faith that his wife Lucille converted to Catholicism. She wanted to share all that was vital to Frank, and she recognized that his Catholicism was Capra's true life force.

If you were to seek a primary theme in Frank Capra's work, it would be resurrection. Frank sincerely believed that only through dying to ourselves can we be triumphant. He saw death as conquerable. Any number of times we spoke of death—never with fear, but always as a rite of passage to a newer and richer and fuller life. (Mind you, he didn't want to die, life was so brimming with possibilities. Frank had a sister who lived to be ninety-six and that to him sounded about right for checking out. He almost made that magic number!)

In a letter to me written in 1978, Frank highlighted the vocation of Christian living. And for him it was to align ourselves with the poor, the broken and the needy. Wrote Capra: "Christ loved the poor, 'Come unto me all ye that are heavy laden'. . . and despised the pompous rich whom He called 'whitened sepulchers which devour widows' houses, and for a pretense make long prayers.' God loves us, Jim, for carrying on His work—the work of Christ, the Apostles, Paul, and all the saints and the martyrs."

It's a Wonderful Life, Meet John Doe, Mr. Smith Goes to Washington, Lost Horizon, Mr. Deeds Goes to Town, and *Pocketful of Miracles* are all about death and resurrection. In each movie Capra gives us a man or woman who seems destroyed but in that moment of absolute despair is born again into the richest meaning of life. And that being "born again" doesn't mean that life will be without pain or suffering, but that we'll see our lives through the wondrous prism of Christ's eyes.

In yet another Capra epistle, he wrote what might be his best epitaph: "I believe that the clean, the honest, the moral, the compassionate, and the forgiving are about all that count in this world. All else is emptiness and vanity." In the passing of Frank Capra, our world lost a visionary filmmaker and a true Christian gentleman. Heaven gained a brother of incomparable goodness. Thank you, Frank, for reminding us that life is a precious and irreplaceable gift, a wonderful treasure.

At Capra's funeral Mass, two songs were sung that beautifully reflected this delightful believer. The recessional was

"America the Beautiful." And Capra, the devoted patriot, truly believed the words of that song. But of perhaps greater importance, his Mass opened with "Joyful, joyful we adore thee." And that was Frank. Filled with a love so deep for Christ—a love that he reflected in the joy he lived. Said Capra in 1985, "Our God is a part of all I did." Amen.

Question for Reflection

• Describe how the theme of resurrection is used in any Frank Capra film you have seen.

Prejudice

Let me tell you an embarrassing story. For eight years I lived at St. Agnes Cathedral rectory in Rockville Centre, New York. The building is huge, three floors high. I lived on the top floor. One morning I woke up to celebrate the 7:45 a.m. Mass. As I left my room, I walked into a tall black man in the middle of the corridor. My stomach froze with apprehension. But, wanting to seem unintimidated, I asked the obvious question: "Can I help you?" He replied, in a matter-of-fact style: "I'm looking for the 7:45 Mass." With a spirit and tone of condescension I replied, "Well, they hold that over in church, not in the rectory." I then instructed him to follow me out of the building. I have no idea what occupied his mind as we silently climbed down the stairs, but I know what I was thinking, and it ran something like this: "I better try to walk behind him because he may be armed. A knife or gun could be in his pocket."

We walked silently to the church and then I rudely pointed to a side door with the admonition: "Inside there is where people attend Mass." I was not very nice, and my manner drippingly revealed my prejudice.

The man then said words I'll never forget. "Well, Father, if it's all the same to you, I think I'll attend Mass instead of concelebrating it. By the way, my name is Father Joseph, and I come from Nigeria." My face fell with embarrassment and a bit of shame. This black man, whom I had written off as a potential thief or mugger, was a priest. A gentle soul seeking hospitality in a rectory. A place he thought he might find Christian charity. How wrong he was! Because in me he found all the intolerance, the fear, the prejudice that so many of us learn and live each day.

In those moments before he identified himself as a priest, he was my enemy, a subject of suspicion and derision. Not because of anything he did, but because his skin was darker than mine.

My attitude toward Father Joseph was a sin. It is the sin of racism, and it has been roundly condemned by the Catholic Church for ages. But, seriously, how many of us even think of it as a sin? When was the last time we went to confession and identified our dislike for people of color, or people who worship a different God, or people of a different nationality, as a sin? Truth is, we're fairly indifferent to the human weakness which is racism. We'll confess lying, stealing, cheating, cursing, even drinking too much. We'll identify ourselves as people who commit sexual sin. We'll list specifically how many times we missed weekly Mass. But call ourselves racist? It almost never happens. And yet it is a sin, and one that pervades too many of our lives, mine included.

Father Joseph, thank God, turned out to be a delightful human being. We talked after Mass and I apologized for the attitude I'd demonstrated before Mass. Joseph was kind enough to admit that it's "perfectly human" to be suspicious about a stranger in your home. And while I think Joseph was being very accepting of my prejudice, I suspect that the Lord wants us to be better than "perfectly human." He wants us to accept each other as if every person we meet is Christ.

Questions for Reflection

- If you had been in the position of being confronted by the unfamiliar black man in the corridor, how would you have reacted?

- "Appearances are deceiving." How does that apply here?

Save the World

During Christmas season, most of us channel surf to catch the great film *It's a Wonderful Life*. Directed by Frank Capra and starring Jimmy Stewart, this movie tells the story of George Bailey. George thinks his life is a failure because he has so few visible signs of success. He's unable to offer a financially rich life to his wife and kids. His business just barely keeps its head above water. He attains none of the trappings of power, money or success. By the story's end, though, George is helped to see that his life, because it's been lived for others, is a wonderful life, the truest kind of success.

It's a Wonderful Life is one of film director Steven Spielberg's favorite movies. No surprise, then, that he produced a modern-day Wonderful Life. The difference is that Spielberg tells a real-life George Bailey story in the person of Oskar Schindler.

Oskar Schindler was a German Catholic living through the World War II years, trying to make some big money. He saw the war not as a tragedy but as an opportunity. He knew that businessmen can profit richly from the spoils of war. And so he set out to cash in on the war by opening an enamelware plant in Kracow. As a member of the Nazi party, and as a large bribegiver, Schindler enjoyed the help and support of the occupying Nazi armies. His work force was made up of Jewish prisoners. This had little effect on Schindler at first; he saw the Jews as simply a means toward his desired end: wealth. Gradually, however, Schindler comes to recognize Jewish prisoners as people, as children of God, as humans worthy of love and friendship. This concurrently forces him to open his eyes to the true horror of the holocaust. And it compels him to make a decision: he must save whichever lives he can.

Oskar Schindler convinces his Nazi friends that the 1,200 Jews working in his factory are necessary for the war effort. He protects his Jewish friends by oiling the Nazi warlords with expensive gifts, black market items and money bribes. Schindler uses the millions he has made during the war to "buy" the workers he needs. War's end will find multimillionaire Schindler completely destitute because of his efforts to save Jewish men, women and children.

Schindler's List, the book and movie that tell the story of Oskar Schindler, is a tale of conversion. It helps us to see that every person has the power to make the world a better place. It is particularly important to note that Oskar Schindler was no saint. Unlike St. Maximilian Kolbe, the Polish priest who offered to die in a concentration camp so that a Jewish man might live to support his family, Schindler had no pretensions about his goodness. He had many extramarital affairs, drank heavily and was a worshiper of the almighty buck. His decision to risk everything to save lives was an incredible story of graduated conscience. He simply could not bring himself to turn a blind eye to the inhumanity of humankind. He recognized that he couldn't save everyone, but he could do something. And doing something of value is always better than doing nothing.

Thanks to Oskar Schindler, 1,200 Jewish people survived the death camps: twelve hundred people who went on to raise families and tell the story of one Catholic man's goodness. They now call themselves "Schindler Jews," and they honor this man of conscience. Schindler died in 1974, penniless and yet incredibly wealthy—because he knew the fullest meaning of the Talmud when it says: "Whoever saves one life, saves the entire world."

Oskar Schindler, a modern-day George Bailey, is buried in Israel in the Catholic cemetery on Mount Zion in Jerusalem, surrounded by a people he finally came to see were very much children of God, just like him.

Question for Reflection

- How do you think God would have judged Oskar Schindler at his death in 1974?

Dysfunctional

One day a woman asked to see me. She said she needed to speak about an important fact she had just learned. She was deeply mysterious on the telephone. I wondered what her secret revelation would be. When we finally met she looked like someone who was about to confess the darkest of tales. Leaning forward she peered into my eyes with great intensity. And then she let me have it. "Father," said the good woman, "it has recently become clear to me that I come from a dysfunctional family!" I breathed a sigh of relief. So that was the horrible revelation. I leaned back and told this nervous lady an equally dark insight: "So do I." Then, as she looked at me with genuine surprise, I gave her the really big news: "So do most people."

It's very trendy these days to call families that don't have it all together "dysfunctional." And the word means what it says—that something (namely, our families) is not performing as it should. It surprises me that this fact shocks so many people. I don't believe that dysfunction is something new. Adam and Eve had a dysfunctional family. All of us have a need to improve family life. All of us can work at improving communication, at forgiving each other for past hurts, at being more faithful to the people we love, at being more present to each other, at expressing our love more openly. And the failure to be perfect is no sin. It is entirely human to be a "work in progress." And as this word dysfunctional bounces around now more than ever, it's good to accept a simple fact of life— no one's family is perfect. We all need improvement.

There are some families, however, which are more dysfunctional than others. And those are families where not everyone admits or attempts to deal with the obvious problems. So, for example, if a parent is alcoholic and everyone knows it and seeks to get help, except for the drinker, our dysfunction can be heightened. No dysfunction is terminal when a family names the prob-

lem and everyone attempts to work on it. But when anyone opts
to ignore or deny the problem—complete healing is not possible.
Abel may have wanted to establish a more harmonious relationship with his brother Cain. But if Cain only had killing on his
mind, healthy family functioning was not possible.

Sometimes families can solve their own problem, but oftentimes outside help is needed. Asking for the help of a trained
counselor is not a sign of weakness but of strength. It takes
courage to admit our problems and to deal with them effec-
tively. The woman who came to see me was well on her way to
a solution. She was naming the family as "in need." If that's all
she did, there'd be problems aplenty. But she went further and
got the help of a professional counselor. Her family dysfunction began to fade as they learned together to work toward
good mental and emotional health.

If you read through the Gospels, you have to be impressed
by the radical honesty of Jesus. He called it as he saw it, and his
forthrightness compelled people to grow. Naming our weakness is a sign of God's power working through our human
pride. And when we do something with our dysfunction,
we're indicating a true maturity.

Once I accompanied a friend to an open meeting of
Alcoholics Anonymous. I went not knowing what to expect. I
found a force for good. I found people doing well because I
found people who were being honest about who they are.

At Alcoholics Anonymous meetings anyone can speak. But
when you begin, you start by identifying the reason you're
there. So, most say: "Hi, my name is _____ and I'm an alcoholic." What's refreshing about this is that no one reacts nega-
tively. Everyone in the meeting accepts the disease, the burden
carried by each speaker.

Listening to the freedom of expression demonstrated by
these courageous people got me to thinking. Can you imagine

how healthy we'd all be if we could freely identify our human weaknesses and learn to deal with them openly? I suspect our dysfunctions would diminish if we could simply name them without fear. "Hell, my name is _____, and I am insensitive, or manipulative, or explosive, or unkind, or unfaithful, or demanding, or ungrateful, or self-centered," or any one of a million dysfunctions we hide. And the more we keep them closeted, the more they fester. Being a dysfunctional person is no sin, but failing to face and admit and deal with your dysfunctions is just plain foolish.

Questions for Reflection

- Why do some family members "opt to ignore or deny" a serious family problem?
- Can you name some instances in your own family in which a problem was ignored? was admitted, and help sought?
- "It is entirely human to be a 'work in progress.'" What does that mean?

Going to Church

I was heading over to church one Sunday morning to help with Communion. When I got to the sacristy, I realized that the priest celebrating Mass was just completing his homily. So I decided to take a walk outside and catch some of the terrific weather we were enjoying.

As I shot out a side door I bumped into two sheepish teenage guys who were obviously into "cutting out." They clutched in their hands copies of the parish bulletin: parental notification of the fact that they had "been to Mass." "Busy day?" I asked them. "No," said the honest older boy, "we're just bored."

This all took me back to the memory of a friendship enjoyed for over 20 years. Some time before one of my closest friends, Joe, went to the Lord, we were considering the elements that kept us good friends over all the years. It wasn't excitement: sometimes we bore each other. It wasn't intellectual: sometimes our conversations were dull beyond belief. It wasn't the richness of our personalities: we both could be annoying, obnoxious and difficult to be around. It wasn't power or money: we didn't have any. In fact, it wasn't friendship based on anything more than our desire to be loyal, to be committed, and to be there for each other.

And friendship, I think, is at the heart of our God-life, too. Sometimes going to church can be boring, dull and intellectually vacant. And if we're going to Mass expecting an exciting floor show, we'll surely be disappointed. Rather, we're there because our friend Jesus has invited us to be there. If we're true friends, we'll take that invitation seriously. That means we'll face and reject all the nonsense we use as excuses for staying away, like:

"I'm really busy." There are 168 hours in every week. We somehow find the time to eat, to sleep, to go to school or work, to play sports and go to the gym, to be with people we care about. In fact, we find or make the time for anything we really believe is important. If our friend Jesus and his people are important, we'll make the time to be there.

"But the homilies are so boring." Give me a break. If we switched off everyone and everything that's boring in life, we'd all stay home in bed. The priest is trying. He may not be great, but at least he's giving it his best. Shouldn't we try to listen? And more to the point: we're not just there for the homily. We go to be part of a community who need us and miss us when we're absent. We go to receive the Body of Christ, who never bores us (or gives up on us).

"Look, I can find God in many places, I don't need a church building to pray." That's true. But let's be honest: if you don't go to church, how much serious praying do you really do? And further, where (outside of church) can you go to receive Communion? Are they giving it out someplace else? More importantly, Jesus told us in no uncertain terms: I want you to gather with other believers to celebrate my life. That means church.

"I used to go, but I had a really bad experience at church."

We have all had some bad experience of church. But again, let's compare our experience of God's friendship with the rest of our lives. If every time you had a poor experience with your mother, your father, your sister, your brother, your friends, you said, "That's it, this relationship's over," we'd have no relationships at all. But we keep at relationships that matter. We forgive, we compromise and we try to love again. Any relationship worth having is worth working on. Why not give the same energy to our love of God and His church as we give to our friends and family?

Question for Reflection

- What excuse have you used or heard most often for not going to church?

Why a Priest?

It usually happens when people start to get comfortable. Feeling relaxed around a priest, folks get the courage they've been meaning to muster for a long time. In a nice but standard refrain, every priest faces "The Question."

It goes like this: "So, Father, tell me, why did you decide to become a priest?" Behind the question is another unspoken interrogative. If it were asked, it might go like this: "So, Father, you seem pretty normal, you're a likeable fellow, you could probably lead a decent life for yourself, why do you want to waste your time doing something so old-fashioned, archaic, and non-contemporary. Because, let's face it, that's how most young people view the priesthood. And the evidence of that attitude is in the lines that aren't forming outside our seminaries. Careers in medicine, law, dentistry, government, accounting and retail continue to attract young persons. But the lifestyle of the priest is chosen by fewer and fewer individuals.

Maybe part of the reason for the lack of interest has something to do with a lack of knowledge. As one teenager put it to me recently: "After you guys say Mass, what else do you do all day?" He really didn't know. So, let me tell you. We visit sick people in hospitals and at home. We bring them the Eucharist. We counsel people with all sorts of pains and problems—some have marriages that are on the rocks; some have problems with their children; some have problems with their parents; some are addicted to alcohol, or drugs, or sex; some just want to go to confession. We visit children in schools and CCD. We go to a lot of meetings—some social, some civic, some spiritual, some educational. All of them long! We pray and we celebrate Mass.

We listen and try to heal. We help to get people married. We help to say goodbye to the dead by assisting the living with their grief. We get in between people who are fighting and try to make peace. We help to feed the poor and shelter the homeless. We answer a lot of mail, and even more phone calls. Some priests (pastors) have mega financial responsibilities, so they worry about how to pay for the parish or school or office bills. We proclaim the word of God and try to make the Lord's message understandable for contemporary people.

Most of my friends didn't become priests. Most have other careers and have chosen the vocation of marriage and family life. They, too, face many challenges and a regularly exhausting schedule.

On the face of it, it may look like a priest "gives up" a family life for the sake of his priesthood. But that's really an incomplete vision of celibacy. Celibacy does mean being chaste. It does mean remaining unmarried and deciding not to raise your own children. But it also means that the freedom from marriage and family life is a freedom to know, love and serve all the families you meet who are in need. You belong to many families. Celibacy is not a lack of family life but an invitation to love even more widely the people you come to know through priesthood.

Sometimes friends ask me if this is "satisfying" or "enough." Often I respond by asking them the same question. All of our lives involve compromise. When we travel down one path we necessarily choose not to go down other (also attractive) paths. And the path called priesthood is a beautiful, challenging, loving, painful, fun-filled, upsetting and yet satisfying road to run. Some folks ask a very obvious question: If priesthood is such a wonderful life, why aren't a lot more people choosing to live it?

It's a good question. There are probably many answers. In today's society, if I asked you what a "successful" person has, there would probably be two main answers: money and sexual intimacy. Our cultural heroes, our stars, our models, are all people with bucks and sexual success. Money and sex are modern-day gods. We're impressed by movie stars who often have no socially redeeming value, but who score big in the cash and sex department. And if these are, in fact, signs of modern-day success, then why would anyone want to become a priest? We're not big in the money department and (hopefully) even poorer when it comes to sexual prowess. No, the priest is called to stand against the tide of what the world calls success. He pulls us back to look again at what really matters in life. He reminds us that faith, compassion, forgiveness, gentleness, fidelity and truth are what really matter. All the rest is just so much fluff.

So why, then, would a normal, healthy, and contemporary person long to be a priest?

To be a giver and not a taker. To leave the world just a little better than he found it. To recognize that this world is not the whole story. To prod good people to be better. To challenge bad people to give it up. To love without counting the cost. To be a part of every family while calling none his own. To remember, in a world rich with temptation, that we are called by the simple carpenter from Nazareth to serve and not be served. In short, our Credo might well read:

"I expect to pass through this world but once. Any good therefore that I can do, or any kindness that I can show to any fellow creature, let me do it now. . . . For I shall not pass this way again."

Questions for Reflection

- "Celibacy is not a lack of family life but an invitation to love even more widely the people you come to know through priesthood." In what concrete ways do you imagine a priest can live this out?

- "If priesthood is such a wonderful life, why aren't a lot more people choosing to live it?" What are your answers to this?

Changes

Father Charles Murphy and Father Frank Dobson were parish priests in St. Thomas the Apostle Church. That's the community in which I grew up. Father Murphy lived and worked in St. Thomas parish for over twenty-five years, Father Dobson for over twenty-two years. For those of us who attended church and school at St. Thomas the Apostle parish, these men were Church for us. They baptized all newborns; they counseled the troubled; they anointed the sick; they visited our homes for blessings and dinners; they buried our loved ones; they were the very fabric of what it meant to be a part of St. Thomas the Apostle parish.

Times have certainly changed. These good priests are home with God, and the long-term assignments they lived are a thing of the past. For while Church leaders back then obviously saw a value to lengthy assignments in the same parish, that's not the thinking now. Dioceses now seem to hold that priests should have a variety of assignments. The value of this diversity is to broaden the varied needs of the Church. I think it's also to keep priests from going a little bit stale. New challenges bring a broadening of our vision and our ability to stay new. The basic diocesan assignment is now for about five years. It can be extended if the priest involved, in consultation with his bishop and the Priest Personnel Board, think that wise and helpful.

Most priests, I suspect, find the variety of assignments an enriching experience. But even admitting that value, there is no denying the discomfort of being uprooted. Priests enter a parish knowing almost no one in the community. But in the course of their assignments, priests come to share great intimacy with their people. We share those moments in life which are treasured forever in the human heart. Baptisms, weddings, first communions, confirmations and funerals are sacred times. Times spent in confession are privileged moments in which people trust their priest with the innermost secrets of their souls. Every priest I know has spent countless hours offering counsel and comfort in the parish offices. Every kind of human pain is shared. We are offered entrance into the lives of our people that goes well beyond psychological counseling.

And then come transfers. The priest is expected to let go of people he has served and to be open to new people, new situations, new challenges. For the people he leaves, there's an ache in seeing someone we cared about move on. And for the priest, there's the frustration of letting go. Some people complain that "Father Mike used to be here, we were very close, but now we don't hear from him anymore." Folks can make it sound like "Father Mike" is somehow callous to the precious times of the past. Nothing could be further from the truth. Father Mike loves his past but is committed to a lifetime of service, wherever that may lead.

So how should we respond to the news that a favorite priest is leaving the parish? Well, to begin with, let him know that he made a difference for the good. Affirm him, encourage him, express the affection you feel. Priests aren't born with leather skin. They need to know they did a good job just like everyone else. Keep him in your prayers, and know that your pain in letting him go is no different from the sorrow he feels in having to move on. Stay in touch, but leave him free enough to do the new job he's been given. Friendship is not about possession; it's about loving freely and then letting my friend go so that he can become all that God destined him to become.

Questions for Reflection

- How did you feel when a popular priest was transferred out of your parish?
- How do you think a priest feels when he is transferred from a parish he likes?

Gospel Fire

A while back a friend invited me to meet several players on the New York Jets football team. We had a fascinating evening together sharing thoughts and insights about God, organized religion and the role of the Spirit in directing our lives.

One particular fact about these players intrigued me. They had, earlier in their lives, been raised Roman Catholics. Now, when I asked them what Church they professed, their answer was simply "Christian." By that they meant they were born again or fundamentalist Christians. For them the Bible and a "spirit-filled" celebration of Jesus are everything.

I listened carefully to their reasons for leaving the Catholic Church. And while I think they "jumped ship" unnecessarily, the pro-ball players made some sense.

Like many people in and out of the Church, they complained that Catholic "preaching" was boring. They wondered why the word of God wasn't presented in a more exciting way. And they have a point. Oftentimes, when I'm on vacation in a distant place, I attend Mass as a layperson. And, quite frankly, sometimes I wonder how the local parishioners put up with the pap they're fed. It seems to me that there are, at least, five weaknesses in preaching we need to examine:

(1) *Being contemporary.* The stories we find in the Scriptures are not just meaningful for the times of Christ. They pulsate with "today" connections, if we just bother to see them. An example—the most often condemned sin in our Lord's time was hypocrisy, being a fraud. If we just retell the Gospels without making a today connection, we're storytellers of ancient tales—not homilists.

(2) *Be understood.* We can, as preachers, sometimes feel the need to overintellectualize the Gospel messages. Our Lord was no snob. He spoke clearly and to the point. He was understood by the simple and by the intellectuals. When we preach we should be understood by the guy with a Ph.D. and his grandfather who never finished grammar school.

(3) *Be truthful, not popular.* Many of us suffer from terminal "nice-guyness." We want the masses to love us so we say many "nice" things. We're not called by Jesus to be nice-sayers. We're called to tell the truth. So, if an issue needs to be addressed, regardless of the controversy, we should proclaim instead of whimper. Racism, abortion, promiscuity, infidelity, drug abuse, spouse abuse and insensitivity to the poor aren't going to go away unless they get challenged.

(4) *Get excited!* When I see someone with enthusiasm, I know they care. When I see someone who looks bored, I yawn too. Our preaching is rooted in the Gospel. It's a Gospel that "shocked" the apostles into action. When we preach without excitement or conviction, we betray the very truth we utter. We need more Gospel fire!

(5) *Be remembered.* The ultimate litmus test for effective preaching may be within our listeners' memory. If we ask our parishioners an hour after we've preached, what they heard, we may have our answer. Many will not remember a blessed word. And they'll be embarrassed that they forgot. The embarrassment should be ours. We are not Chinese food. And our listeners shouldn't be hungry so soon after feeding. We are called to feed them with a feast that keeps them nourished, challenged, uncomfortable, questioning and compelled to action.

My sports companions still belong inside the Catholic Church. Their exit was premature. But we can help to keep others inside the Church by caring to give the very best.

Questions for Reflection

- How important do you think the homily is to the meaningfulness of a Mass?
- What can you do to help your parish priests be better preachers?

Dare We Pray?

Several years ago I did something that would be against the law today. The folks who run our local public high school asked me to say a prayer at graduation. I agreed, with the understanding that the prayer would be general in nature and inclusive in approach. I realized that not only Catholic students would be present, but Jews, Protestants, Greek Orthodox and some who believed in no organized religion. The prayer didn't seem to offend anyone. It simply asked the "Creator of life to bless us, bless our families and grant us the wisdom to use ourselves in service to others." But today I would be banned from praying any such prayer at a public school graduation, because courts have ruled that invoking a deity may offend the religious sensitivities of nonbelievers.

Personally, I find such logic very much off the mark. Words, spoken to a Creator are unlikely to damage anyone. For believers, they offer comfort and encouragement. And it's stretching it, I think, to suggest that nonbelievers are going to be bothered by a few moments of praise to God. The courts, regarding prayer in school, have gone even further. They've banned even a short period of silent prayer. It had been suggested that to respect individual conscience, school should start with a period of meditative silence. If people wanted to pray to their God, they could do that. But if they wanted to simply meditate on their next homework assignment, that was their business. But even this suggestion was shot down out of fear that somebody might actually be praying in a tax-supported public institution!

What, we might wonder, is everybody afraid of? Our currency reads, "In God We Trust," and still the nation stands. Our Congress regularly opens with a generic prayer offered by a chaplain, and the nation still stands. Surveys indicate that over 90 percent of our citizens believe in God. So why, then, in this wonderful democracy are we afraid to let young people pause for a moment of silent prayer? What is it we're protecting them from?

And, God knows, we can certainly use all the prayers we can muster. The incidences of violent crimes, out-of-wedlock births, and divorces in the United States continue to climb. The number of children being raised by a single parent has tripled. The teenage suicide rate has also tripled. All this has occurred as the courts continue to "protect" us from the perceived dangers of private prayer in public institutions.

So let me make a suggestion to students at every level of the educational system: Pray anyway. This is not a totalitarian state. No one can control your mind. No one can tell you what to think or pray about. They can ban people like me from saying a prayer, but they can't ever stop you from reflecting on the greatness of God. And you can do it anywhere you choose. Yes, even in the public school classroom or cafeteria.

And, speaking of prayer, let's try to do it more consistently. Most of us, I suspect, are still running to God to play "let's make a deal." We turn to our Creator when we want or need something. We make him promises. If he'll give us this, we'll deliver that. But such prayer presumes that there are some moments in which God doesn't already know and care about our best interests. And those moments simply don't exist. God always knows what's good for us, and we don't have to treat him like a buyer or a trader. But it would be nice if our prayer was for nothing in particular. It would be great if we could just, every day, say prayers of thanks and praise for the gifts of life and love we too often take for granted.

When you love someone, those feelings are often understood without words. But words are terrific, and hearing them tends to make us feel even more deeply loved. God loves our messages of caring. And whether we utter them publicly or in the privacy of our hearts, God treasures them as he treasures us: completely and without conditions.

Questions for Reflection

- Why, or to what extent, might the statistics cited in paragraph 4 be attributed to the absence of prayer in schools?

- There are social pressures to be "pro-choice" when it comes to abortion, yet "pro-choice" where prayer is concerned is frowned upon. Do you see any inconsistencies here?

Prince of Peace

Ben Kingsley is an actor best known for his sterling portrayal in the title role of the movie *Gandhi*. For it he received the Academy Award as Best Actor. Since that early 1980s film, Kingsley has given a number of provocative performances in features like *Bugsy, Maurice, Betrayal, Searching for Bobby Fischer* and *Sneakers*. One of his most poignant portrayals was as Itzhak Stern in Spielberg's *Schindler's List*. In an effort to promote this incredibly challenging movie, Kingsley granted a number of interviews.

In light of *Schindler's List's* focus on the devastation of anti-Semitism, I asked Kingsley about his personal experiences with prejudice. He is, after all, the son of an Indian father (Kingsley's original name was Krishna Bhanji) and a British mother. Certainly, I suspected, he must have known the sting of bigotry earlier in his life. But Kingsley, while thoughtful, intellectual and soulful, is also terribly private. He told me that an actor acts, and that the character of Stern had nothing to do with him personally. In other words, the personal road is closed. Being a bit more persistent than I had planned, I pressed him. "Religion seems to fuel so much hatred in our world, you must have some personal insight into the why of that," I asked. Kingsley's eyes narrowed, his voice rose and he revealed his ideas about intolerance. "Because religion is no longer a spiritual experience. Religion has been manipulated into a political weapon. If religion has caused hatred in the world, it's no longer religion, it has become politics."

Consider the truth of Kingsley's perspective. He played Gandhi, a Hindu whose people have long warred with neighboring Muslims. Consider Iraq and Iran where hundreds of thousands have died in a "holy war." Consider Northern Ireland, where all parties profess that they worship Jesus Christ, the Prince of Peace, but who are incapable of offering his peace to one another. Consider the Eastern Orthodox Serbs who routinely slaughter their Catholic Croatian neighbors or their Muslim compatriots. Consider over a thousand years of Christian hatred for the Jews, even though the center of the Christian faith was himself a practicing Jew. Consider the culmination of that hatred, the Holocaust, and the fact that, Christians (oftentimes themselves the victims) cooperated in exterminating over six million Jews in Europe. Consider the Greeks who profess to believe in Jesus, but who detest the children of Islam living next door in Turkey. Consider our fundamentalist Christian brothers and sisters, working avidly to convert the Catholics of South America by telling them that the Pope is an anti-Christ and that theirs is the only "true" Christian faith.

Yes, in the name of God we do divide, kill, conquer and destroy. But are any of these really manifestations of religion? Not at all. In none of these faiths is killing, destroying, dividing or conquering encouraged. In fact, just the opposite is true. Each of the faiths I've mentioned encourages peace, love, community, and forgiveness. So how, then, do we taint these roads of faith into avenues of hatred? By, I suspect, doing precisely what Ben Kingsley condemned: making religion serve politics instead of transforming politics because of our religion. Politics is a very human response to problems with other human beings. But it lacks any spiritual dimension to transform, to uplift or to convert. That's where religion comes in; that's where religion holds special value. Because, when doing its proper job, religion looks politics in the eyes and says, "You've made a real mess of this world; why not try a little faith and love, a little compassion and forgiveness instead?"

Ben Kingsley was right. There's nothing wrong with religion, it is a force for incredible good. But only if it's lived free from the corruption of the anti-spiritual powers of this world.

Question for Reflection

- In what concrete ways can we transform politics by means of our religion?

Additional Titles Published by Resurrection Press, a Catholic Book Publishing Imprint

A Rachel Rosary *Larry Kupferman*	$4.50
A Season in the South *Marci Alborghetti*	$10.95
Blessings All Around *Dolores Leckey*	$8.95
Catholic Is Wonderful *Mitch Finley*	$4.95
Days of Intense Emotion *Keeler/Moses*	$12.95
The Edge of Greatness *Joni Woelfel*	$9.95
Feasts of Life *Jim Vlaun*	$12.95
From Holy Hour to Happy Hour *Francis X. Gaeta*	$7.95
5-Minute Miracles *Linda Schubert*	$4.95
Grace Notes *Lorraine Murray*	$9.95
Healing through the Mass *Robert DeGrandis, SSJ*	$9.95
Heart Peace *Adolfo Quezada*	$9.95
How Shall We Pray? *James Gaffney*	$5.95
The Joy of Being an Altar Server *Joseph Champlin*	$5.95
The Joy of Being a Catechist *Gloria Durka*	$4.95
The Joy of Being a Eucharistic Minister *Mitch Finley*	$5.95
The Joy of Being a Lector *Mitch Finley*	$5.95
The Joy of Being an Usher *Gretchen Hailer, RSHM*	$5.95
The Joy of Music Ministry *J.M. Talbot*	$6.95
The Joy of Praying the Rosary *James McNamara*	$5.95
The Joy of Preaching *Rod Damico*	$6.95
The Joy of Teaching *Joanmarie Smith*	$5.95
The Joy of Worshiping Together *Rod Damico*	$5.95
Life, Love and Laughter *Jim Vlaun*	$7.95
Lights in the Darkness *Ave Clark, O.P.*	$8.95
Love and Hope *Robert E. Lauder*	$8.95
Loving Yourself for God's Sake *Adolfo Quezada*	$5.95
Meditations for Survivors of Suicide *Joni Woelfel*	$8.95
Mother O' Mine *Harry W. Paige*	$9.95
Mother Teresa *Eugene Palumbo, S.D.B.*	$5.95
Mourning Sickness *Keith Smith*	$8.95
Our Grounds for Hope *Fulton J. Sheen*	$7.95
Praying Our Grief *Linda Rooney*	$5.95
Praying the Lord's Prayer with Mary *Muto/vanKaam*	$8.95
Reaching Out *Joseph Lynch*	$9.95
Sabbath Moments *Adolfo Quezada*	$6.95
Season of New Beginnings *Mitch Finley*	$4.95
Sometimes I Haven't Got a Prayer *Mary Sherry*	$8.95
St. Katharine Drexel *Daniel McSheffery*	$12.95
What He Did for Love *Francis X. Gaeta*	$5.95
Woman Soul *Pat Duffy, OP*	$7.95
You Are My Beloved *Mitch Finley*	$10.95

For a free catalog call 1-800-892-6657
www.catholicbookpublishing.com